FUNNY SHORTS

TEN COMIC PLAYS

VOLUME 1

Printed in the United States of America
First Printing, 2020
ISBN 9798590637379

John McDonnell Publishing
39 Doyle Street
Doylestown, PA 18901
www.johnfmcdonnell.com

WHAT THEY'RE SAYING ABOUT *FUNNY SHORTS...*

As a master of the short play form, John McDonnell holds up a mirror to the way we live now. Always revealing, always spot on, and always very funny, his plays are a dream for actors. Easy to produce—they work as well on a bare stage as they do in a fully realized production. Either way, the audiences are always entertained and leave the theatre happier than when they came in. You will enjoy reading or performing the works of John McDonnell.

—John Augustine is a playwright, television writer, actor and director. He has taught playwriting in New York City at Playwrights Horizons Theatre School, The 42nd Street Collective, NYU, and at Sarah Lawrence College.

Every theatre instructor needs that absolutely infallible book of scenes for students. John McDonnell's plays are full of hilarious reveals and quirky character studies, with plot twists that provide actors with meaningful discussion about motivation, foreshadowing, and bold choices.

What's even better? The length of the comic short plays provides significant opportunities for memorization and stage time for everyone involved. This is the perfect comedy collection for your studio classroom!

—Sarah LeClair is the Youth Education Director at Comedy Sportz Philadelphia and a curriculum writer/consultant for The Philadelphia Shakespeare Theatre teaching artist program. Sarah has spent more than twenty years in new play development and performing arts opportunities for community theatres, undergraduate college programs, and high school actors.

John finds the absurd in the mundane, the fracture in the fable. Guaranteed a laugh in every bite!

—Joey Perillo calls himself an erstwhile cab driver, but in reality he's a veteran character actor who has appeared as a principal (speaking) actor in virtually every theatrical medium, including 14 major motion pictures (*Philadelphia, 12 Monkeys, Rachel Getting Married, The Negotiator,* and *The Manchurian Candidate,* among others), and the original (and best) *Hairspray*. He has also appeared as a principal on TV shows like *ER, Hack, Homicide, The Wire,* and *The Sopranos*. Joey is a long-time member of the Screen Actors Guild

and Actors Equity Association.

I have had the pleasure of working as a fellow writer with John in workshop settings, and I have also been fortunate as an actor to appear in a number of his plays. No matter what the set up for the play, his mischievous sense of humor comes through in spades, assuring that people will leave the theatre still laughing and feeling uplifted. Clever dialogue and crazy twists make his plays as much fun for the performers as for the audience. No matter what side of the footlights you're on, you can't help but have a good time at a John McDonnell play.

—Rick Goodwin has degrees in Theater and The Oral Interpretation of Literature from Northwestern University. He has performed a wide range of characters and written numerous plays, including *Home Smarts*, which was a finalist at Manhattan Rep's Spring One-Act Competition in 2018, and the full-length *Bleeding in B&W*, which will be produced at Phillips' Mill in 2021. Rick is a member of the Dramatist's Guild.

It's always an honor to work with John McDonnell, and I've been fortunate to perform many of his short plays. They are always witty, engaging, and relatable. John creates likable characters and gives them dialogue that makes the audience think about the human condition in a hysterical way.

—Dave Levy is an educator, actor, and comedic improvisor. He is the Director of the Summer Youth Workshops at Town and Country Players, Buckingham PA, and has performed in 12 shows at T&C in recent years. In addition, Dave has been involved with New Feathers Productions, Playwright's Bridge workshop group, and Funny Shorts. He is an active performer in a comedic improv troupe called Bucket of Phones.

McDonnell's genius lies in putting his quirky characters into ordinary scenarios and then letting us watch how they react when circumstances go seriously awry. The men and women he gives life to in his plays are both warm and wacky, the kind of people I would love to get to know at a party. He peoples his stories with individuals who consistently refuse to do the expected.

John's Playwrights' Bridge workshop group has done more for both writers and actors than any other group in Bucks County. I was invited to join last year and my writing has benefitted immensely from the feedback I have received from the actors and writers who are members. I only wish I had found this wonderful group sooner.

—Author Lisa DeAngelis's *Angels Unaware* will be published by Regal House in June, 2021.

John's plays are warm, funny, and heartfelt. They are fun to perform because each character has a very strong objective right from the start. I find an inherent goodness and hope in his writing.

—Righteous Jolly is a Circle In The Square Alumnus (2003). His regional credits include: *Sweeney Todd, Jesus Christ Superstar, Orphans* (Phillip), *Marvin's Room* (Hank), *Mirette* (Bellini) *Bloody Bloody Andrew Jackson* (Andrew Jackson), *Mamma Mia* (Sam Carmichael). Film, TV, & Web: Robert McKenzie in *Gemini Rising*. Krampus in *Merry Krampus*. Lorenzo de Medici and King Charlemagne in *The Pope: A Mini Series*.

INTRODUCTION

This is my book of funny plays.

I've been a writer for decades, but I didn't write my first play until 2015. That's when I took a playwriting class at the Bucks County Playhouse, in New Hope PA, and in the very first session I wrote a funny scene. There was no deep meaning, no hidden agenda—it was just two lions having a conversation about what to eat for lunch. I laughed as I wrote it, my classmates laughed when they read it, and I kept writing comedies after that.

I entered my plays in theater festivals across the country, and many were selected—so far, my plays have been performed at theaters in New Mexico, Alabama, Washington, Pennsylvania, Michigan, and New Jersey.

And I couldn't be happier.

After all, what's better than giving people a good laugh? Not much, especially lately, when the world has seemed especially grim and serious. If ever we needed a good belly laugh it's now, when just checking your news feed on your phone is liable to give you a panic attack.

And that's how I got the idea for this book. I wanted to share my plays with more people, and there's no better way to do that than to self-publish a book. I picked ten of my most popular short plays and put them in this book so people can read them and get a laugh. And after they stop laughing, they might just decide they want to see them performed.

Which is great! My plays are perfect for performances, whether in person or through livestreaming, on a podcast, an audio play, or other venues. There are no rigid requirements about costumes, sets, lighting, or anything else. The dialogue is not complicated, and there are no physical demands on the actors.

These plays work well for student drama classes or productions, community theaters, senior centers— really, just about any type of production you can think of.

Want to put my plays on? My fee is reasonable—$20 for each play. I charge the $20 fee for performance rights to each play up to five, and $60 for a group of six plays or more. Just email me at mcdonnellwrite@gmail.com and we'll work out the details. By the way, that's a one-time permission: if you're interested in the rights to multiple performances, email me for more information.

Note: Even with my permission you must credit me as the author in any advertising or promotional material. I'll be happy to promote your performance on my social media if you give me the details. If you need a PDF copy of the plays for your actors, let me know and I'll send it to you for a fee of $20 per play. All you need to do is send me an email—mcdonnellwrite@gmail.com.

PLEASE UNDERSTAND, I AM NOT GIVING PERMISSION FOR ANYONE TO REPRINT MY PLAYS, PUBLISH THEM FOR SALE IN ANY FORMAT, OR SELL VIDEO OR AUDIO RECORDINGS OF THEM.

If you have any questions, comments, or suggestions, let me know. And by the way, I LOVE getting feedback on my plays! By all means, let me know what your audience thinks.

Thank you for buying a copy of *Funny Shorts*. I know you're going to get a good laugh from these plays.

And that's something we all need these days!

John McDonnell

PUBLISHER STATEMENT

FICTITIOUS DISCLAIMER

This book is a work of fiction. Any similarity between the characters and situations within its pages and places or persons, living or dead, is unintentional and co-incidental.

DEDICATION

To my wife Anita. Thanks for all the laughter.

Table of Contents

PUNISHMENT CARD

CHARACTERS

MR. WILLIAMS   A shopper at Tidy Stores. He is
                      around 50.

AUDRA   A manager at Tidy Stories. She
WALLOP   is around 40.

ALF   The Punishment Manager at
SLEDGECOCK   Tidy Stores. He is wearing a
                      Santa hat.

SETTING

Audra Wallop's office. She is sitting across a desk from Mr. Williams, a customer. She has a computer on her desk, and she looks at it from time to time.

TIME

Present.

AUDRA

Hello Mr. Williams, my name is Audra Wallop. You're probably wondering why I called you into my office.

MR. WILLIAMS

Yes I am, actually. I just came in to purchase some wrapping paper. I don't know why the young woman at the register told me to come back here.

AUDRA

Well, she scanned your card, you see.

MR. WILLIAMS

I know. She told me there was some irregularity.

AUDRA

Yes. It seems, Mr. Williams, that you've been doing your Christmas shopping somewhere else this year.

MR. WILLIAMS

Well, I, uh, suppose I've—

AUDRA

Been going to the Buxom.com Web site, have you?

MR. WILLIAMS

Just for a small item or two. Not anything, you know, big. The big orders, I always come here.

AUDRA

Do you? I see. You haven't been to the Buxom.com site recently to buy, oh, a new laptop and video games for your son, a digital camera for your daughter, some earrings for your wife, and a super deluxe Lego set for your nephew, for a grand total of, let's see — $3,500?

MR. WILLIAMS

Uh, maybe. Well, I guess so. Yes, now that you mention it, I did spend a bit more there last week. It was just a one-time thing.

AUDRA

A bit more? So, $3,500 is a bit more, eh? And you say this was just a one-time thing?

MR. WILLIAMS

Oh, yes. Yes, that was unusual for me. I rarely shop online at Christmastime.

AUDRA

Hmm. That's not what I see on my screen, Mr. Williams. It seems you've been visiting Buxom.com a lot lately. In fact, you've been shopping there more than here. And you're spending quite a healthy little sum with them! I see you're almost at $4,000 for the month.

MR. WILLIAMS

Is that so? Four thousand? I didn't realize it was that much.

AUDRA

Oh it is. And do you know what that means, Mr. Williams?

MR. WILLIAMS

No, I don't.

AUDRA

It means you've accumulated a thousand points on your punishment card.

MR. WILLIAMS

Punishment card? What punishment card? I don't have a punishment card.

AUDRA

Actually you do. It's the same as your rewards

card. It has a running balance, you see, and it subtracts punishment points from rewards points, so that if a customer does what you've been doing—buying from an online competitor—they can have a large negative balance.

MR. WILLIAMS

Negative balance? I didn't know you kept numbers like that.

AUDRA

Didn't read the fine print at the bottom of your card, I take it?

MR. WILLIAMS

No, I didn't. I thought it was just a regular rewards card.

AUDRA

chuckling

No, we've moved far beyond rewards cards, Mr. Williams. It's a new world out there in retail, and we've had to adapt.

MR. WILLIAMS

Yes, I've heard the competition is fierce these days.

AUDRA

Fierce? Oh, you have no idea, Mr. Williams. That's why punishment cards are the new thing. They help us to build a stronger relationship with our customers. You might say they add muscle to our loyalty program.

MR. WILLIAMS

Well, I don't think that's very nice, giving punishment points to customers. It seems rather rude, if you want my opinion.

AUDRA

Rude? We take a different view of that. We think it's a bit rude when customers that we've spent time and money nurturing for many years take their business elsewhere. We like to think of ourselves as your best friend, Mr. Williams. How would you feel if you found out your best friend was buying all of his expensive Christmas presents from your arch-enemy's Web site, and he was coming to you only to buy wrapping paper? How would that make you feel? No, we've had our hearts broken too many times by customers, Mr. Williams. Tidy Stores is now taking action with gigolos like you.

MR. WILLIAMS
insulted

Gigolos? I really don't know what you mean. I've been a very faithful customer over the years. Just because I go to a Web site once in a while...this is the 21st century, Mrs. Wallop—everybody does it. But, I don't have time to sit here and discuss this. I have to be going.

(starts to get up).

AUDRA
Not so fast, Mr. Williams, not so fast.

MR. WILLIAMS
What do you mean?

AUDRA
You haven't received your punishment.

MR. WILLIAMS
Punishment? What are you talking about?

AUDRA
We just discussed your punishment balance, remember? You've accumulated quite a lot of punishment points, and since it's the end of the month, it's time for your punishment.

MR. WILLIAMS
My punishment? I didn't think you were serious. What kind of punishment?

AUDRA
Oh, we'll figure that out.

Alf Sledgecock appears at the door.

AUDRA
Ah, there's Mr. Sledgecock now! Mr. Williams, meet Alf Sledgecock.

ALF *(enters)*
'ello, Mr. Williams.

MR. WILLIAMS
I don't understand. Who are you?

ALF
The name is Alf Sledgecock, sir, at your service!

AUDRA
Mr. Sledgecock is our Punishment Manager.

MR. WILLIAMS
Punishment Manager? You've got to be kidding.

AUDRA
(chuckles)

No, I'm not kidding, Mr. Williams. Mr. Sledgecock is here to give you your punishment.

ALF

Nice to meet you, sir. Now, if we could just get down to business.

MR. WILLIAMS

Wh-what are you going to do?

ALF

We'll get to that, sir, don't you worry. 'ow many points does Mr. Williams 'ave, Mrs. Wallop?

AUDRA *(looks at her screen)*

Well, as of right this minute he has accumulated one thousand punishment points. He's been a bad boy lately, shopping at Buxom.com.

ALF

Is that so? Oh, that's naughty, sir, that's very naughty. Shopping at Buxom.com? We can't 'ave that, can we?

MR. WILLIAMS
Getting nervous

I didn't realize. I only thought I'd buy a few things. You know how it is, you go to a Web site for one item, you see half a dozen other products you need. They make it so easy! It's a temptation, and I guess I don't have enough will power to resist.

ALF
But that's why you shouldn't have gone there in the first place, you see! We have to retaliate when you do that. It's company policy, sir.

MR. WILLIAMS
I didn't know! I swear I didn't know!

AUDRA
Mr. Williams didn't read the fine print on his card.

ALF
Now, isn't that a pity? Yes, it's always the fine print that gets you. I feel for you, sir, I really do. But that doesn't change what I 'ave to do.

MR. WILLIAMS
Wh-what do you have to do?

ALF

In good time, sir, in good time. I just have to ask a question or two. Make things all proper and professional, if you know what I mean. I'm your man for following procedures, I am! Are you right 'anded or left 'anded, sir?

MR. WILLIAMS

I'm right handed. Why do you need to know that?

ALF

Very good sir, very good. Now, be a good lad and hold out your left 'and, will you? That way we won't have a problem when you need to sign your debit slips, will we?

MR. WILLIAMS

Oh, God! What are you going to do?

ALF

(Chuckling)

You should have thought of that before you shopped at Buxom.com, Mr. Williams. Life takes funny turns, don't it? Ah, I know it's easy to fall for the pretty little online store! I've 'alf a mind to do it myself when I get an email about a delicious sale. You know how they come on to you with all the bright colors and the big letters—"Free shipping!", they'll say. Or, "Buy one, get one free!" But, we mustn't fall for cheap slutty come-ons like that! It's always better to stay loyal to dear old Tidy Stores, isn't it?

MR. WILLIAMS

It was just a passing flirtation, I swear! It meant nothing, nothing! I actually regretted it afterward, you know. I felt cheap, sleazy—even dirty! It's just that they were having all these two for one sales and I got weak. It was Black Friday, and it seemed so exciting! You know how it is—the forbidden fruit, and all that. You understand, don't you? Listen, I'll do better, though, I promise!

ALF

Of course you will, sir, of course you will. Now just hold your hand steady. Yes, that's right. Don't be squeamish, lad. This will only hurt for a week or so.

(He pulls out a hammer).

MR. WILLIAMS

Is that a hammer? What are you doing with a hammer?

AUDRA

Mr. Sledgecock, I'm afraid that won't do. Remember, I said Mr. Williams has a THOUSAND punishment points.

ALF

A thousand punishment points, did you say? Oh, then a hammer won't do at all, will it?

MR. WILLIAMS
Sigh of relief

Thank goodness. For a moment there I thought—

Alf pulls out a baseball bat

ALF

'here we go, Mr. Williams. This should do the trick!

MR. WILLIAMS

No! No, don't do that! Can't you reconsider? I promise I'll shop at your store from now on! No more online shopping for me!

ALF

Now what would the world come to if I did that? Rules are rules, aren't they? When you 'ave a thousand punishment points, why, we 'ave to give you a proper punishment! If I didn't follow the rules lad, it'd be total anarchy. You'd have robots taking over the world, wouldn't you? The bloody computers would be running everything!

MR. WILLIAMS
There must be a solution. There must! Can I buy back the points?

ALF
Ah! Now you're talking! I believe we can do that, can't we Mrs. Wallop?

AUDRA
Why yes, as a matter of fact, we do offer a buyback option. Would you like to do that, Mr. Williams?

MR. WILLIAMS
Yes! Yes! Anything! How much does it cost?

AUDRA
Well, let's see. To buy back a thousand points, that would be five thousand dollars.

MR. WILLIAMS
Five thousand! What? That's outrageous.

That's highway robbery!

AUDRA

I see. Well, then, Mr. Sledgecock, you may proceed.

ALF

Yes, mum. There now, put your 'and out again, sir. It won't take a minute.

MR. WILLIAMS

No! No that's perfectly fine. No problem at all! I just happen to have a checkbook with me. *(pulls out his checkbook)*. I'll write it out now. *(scribbles a check)* Here! There you go.

AUDRA

Good! Thank you Mr. Williams. It's been a pleasure doing business with you.

ALF

Yes, thank you, sir. We're 'appy you see the importance of punishment cards. Loyalty! That's what we're after at Tidy Stores.

MR. WILLIAMS

Oh, yes, I'll be loyal! I'll be very, very loyal, don't you worry about that! I'm going to go home and throw my computer away—I'm getting rid of my high speed Internet connection too! Is it okay for me to leave? I'd really like to leave now.

AUDRA

Of course, Mr. Williams. And remember our store's motto—"Spare the rod and spoil the customer."

MR. WILLIAMS

Oh, I won't forget that! Goodbye! *(He runs out).*

ALF

There's a job well done! It always makes me feel good to see a customer who's learned his lesson. They're not a bad lot, most of them— they just need a little re-education, that's all. Once they realize that good old bricks and mortar can satisfy them more than a Web site, why, they get right back in the Christmas spirit, don't they?

AUDRA

Indeed they do, Mr. Sledgecock, indeed they do.

THE END

TEN MINUTE GRIEF COUNSELING

CHARACTERS

EMILY
WILSON
Around 50 years old. Dressed stylishly. Clearly troubled about something.

FRANCINE
STIGMA
Sixtyish. Looks rather sweet and grandmotherly, but with a steely demeanor that is quickly apparent. She is wearing a Santa Claus hat.

SETTING

A cemetery, on a bench.

TIME

Present. Late afternoon.

Francine is sitting on a bench. There is a sign next to her on an easel. It says, "Grief Counseling, $50 for 10 minutes". Emily approaches her tentatively.

EMILY

Excuse me.

FRANCINE

Yes?

EMILY

Are you the Grief Counselor?

FRANCINE

That's me. Sit down, dear.

EMILY
            (sits down)

I was told you'd be here.

FRANCINE

Yes, I'm here most days.

EMILY
I'm so glad I found you.

FRANCINE
(smiles expectantly)

Well, then, let's get started.

EMILY
My name is Emily Wilson.

FRANCINE
Nice to meet you, Emily. My name is Francine Stigma.

EMILY
Stigma? That's an unusual—

FRANCINE
(businesslike)

Yes, I know. Could we get down to business? Christmas is a week away, and I'm sure I'll have other clients arriving soon. It's a busy time of year for me, as I'm sure you understand.

EMILY
Oh, right. *(Pause).* I'm sorry, but I don't know

how to start.

FRANCINE
Who are you here for? Mother? Father? Husband? Perhaps your pet hamster?

EMILY
My pet hamster? But this isn't a pet cemetery.

FRANCINE
I know, but my clients often have referred grief. They come here to visit Aunt Molly's grave, and the next thing you know they're thinking about the pet hamster they had in third grade, the one the cat ate, and they get so sad. Grief works in strange ways. But I take it that's not your situation.

EMILY
No. It's my mother. She's buried over there. Row 75, Plot 12.

FRANCINE
Yes, I'm familiar with that section. I've had several clients with family over there.

EMILY
She died last spring. Only eight months ago, as a matter of fact.

FRANCINE

I see. And you're feeling a little upset, is that right?

EMILY

Yes. Christmas is coming, and it's just—

FRANCINE

The holidays. I understand.

EMILY

I keep thinking about her last few years in the nursing home. It was terrible.

FRANCINE

Yes, I'm sure it was.

EMILY

Horrible. I would fly in from Minneapolis. . .

FRANCINE

Minneapolis? This is Miami, dear. That's a four and a half hour flight.

EMILY

Yes it is. I made the trip, though. I just had to see her.

FRANCINE

And I bet you came once a week, didn't you?

EMILY

Well, actually, no. Not once a week.

FRANCINE

I see. Was it once every two weeks?

EMILY

No, I can't say it was once every two weeks.

FRANCINE

Well, then. As a rule, was it once every three weeks?

EMILY

No, not really. I had a lot of responsibilities in Minneapolis. I couldn't get away very—

FRANCINE

Once a month? Was it once a month?

EMILY

Yes, I guess that's more like it. About once a month.

FRANCINE

Once a month? Is that right? You came once a

month to see your dying mother?

EMILY
She wasn't dying the whole time. She was just really sick, you see.

FRANCINE
Oh, I see. I see very well. *(pause)*. Yes, *(chuckles)* I can see what's going on here. Next question: Was she sick when you institutionalized her?

EMILY
Sick? Technically no. She was just getting older, that's all. She lived alone, and it worried me so much. I didn't have anyone to check on her, and I was so anxious.

FRANCINE
So she was in the pink of health when you put her in that cold, impersonal—

EMILY
It was a very hard decision for me! I thought it would be for the best. She lived alone, like I said.

FRANCINE
And what were her thoughts about this? About moving into a strange place, where she

didn't know a soul, didn't recognize anything familiar, didn't—

EMILY
Oh, she liked it! There was so much to do. Of course, she missed her house and her friends in the neighborhood.

FRANCINE
How long did she live in her house?

EMILY
Her house? About 35 years.

FRANCINE
Thank you, I have it all clear now. It seems you forced your mother to leave a house she lived in for 35 years, then dumped her in a nursing home against her wishes. Do I have it right?

EMILY
It wasn't "forced". That's not the right word at all. I had a discussion with her. I talked to her about it several times, to get her used to the idea. You could say we had an agreement.

FRANCINE
with an edge to her voice

Agreement. That's an interesting word for what you did. I'm sure your mother could think of other words to describe it.

EMILY

It was very sad, the way she went downhill so fast after I moved her in.

FRANCINE

I bet it was more than sad, Emily. I'd say it was a horror show.

EMILY

Horror show? I wouldn't describe it that way.

FRANCINE

No? How about an abduction, would that be a better way to describe it? Or maybe a kidnapping?

EMILY

Excuse me? That's a pretty extreme way of putting it. Listen, it wasn't a bad place. Friendly Retreat has won awards for its Activities Center. They play bingo, they have jugglers and clowns who come in to entertain them—it's a beautiful place, where the residents are always happy.

FRANCINE

Friendly Retreat? Sounds like a name from a Stephen King novel. And they brought in clowns? Oh, I bet your mother loved having some goofball with a big red nose and a fright wig popping into her room!

EMILY

Now, that's a bit much! Listen, I came here for grief counseling, not to be insulted! I don't know what kind of a grief counselor you are!

FRANCINE

The kind that tells the truth, honey.

EMILY

What? How can you say that? I resent the implication that I'm not a good daughter. I cared about my mother. I came to visit—

FRANCINE
(voice rising)

You came once a month—once a month!—to see your frail, elderly mother, who was sitting there knitting booties all day long.

EMILY

Booties? Why would she be knitting booties?

FRANCINE

They were booties for the grandchild she always hoped you would give her. The grandchild that she prayed for every night, alone in her bed in that cold, heartless nursing home. The grandchild you were too selfish to give her!

EMILY

She couldn't have been knitting booties! She didn't know how to knit!

FRANCINE

Ha, that's what you thought! You didn't know she could knit because you never came to visit her!

EMILY

This is really getting out of hand. I don't know what your point is here.

FRANCINE

My point? My point is you hatched an evil plan to get rid of your mother, a sweet old lady who never said a mean word to anyone except for her friends, and that was just to put them in their places when they got too braggy about their grandchildren. Which, by the way, is an important function for old ladies. Where would our society be if old ladies weren't allowed to be mean? We'd all be too nice to each other, and there'd be no need for religion anymore! Anyway, back to your evil plan. You were too busy with your high and mighty life in Minneapolis, so you dumped your mother in that concentration camp of a nursing home!

EMILY

That's really unfair! Okay, I admit I could have visited a few more times. Maybe that was my fault. It's just, I didn't realize how sick she was.

FRANCINE

You didn't realize? A likely story. Of course she was sick about the way you abandoned her, about the treachery of her one daughter. Why didn't you just shoot her and dump her body in the ocean, like the Mafia? It would have been quicker.

EMILY

I didn't abandon her on purpose! You can't blame me for that!

FRANCINE

Hah! No jury would believe that story. It's a bold-faced lie, that's what it is!

EMILY

(Crumbling) It was too much! Every time I came to see her, she was worse. She didn't even know me after a while!

FRANCINE

She didn't want to know you! You, the betrayer who put her in that living hell of a nursing home where she sat and knitted booties all day for the grandchild that never came. You, who whacked her like a hit man!

EMILY

(Distraught)

I thought I was doing the right thing. I did, I really did!

FRANCINE

I submit that you, Emily Wilson, you killed her! It was your fault she died! Oh, you didn't thrust the knife into her, but your abandonment broke her heart! Of course there was also her unrequited love for the cute young male nurse who worked the night shift, but that's another story. You, Emily Wilson, you killed her! I rest my case.

EMILY

I did, didn't I? I killed her! I'm responsible. Oh, I feel so guilty about it all. I should have done better by her. I failed her.

FRANCINE

(Long pause) I bet it wasn't the first time, was it?

EMILY

No. I failed her all the time. Everything was my fault. Even when I was little, I failed her. I never measured up. Everything she wanted me to do, I screwed up. Do you know she wanted me to be a ballerina? I couldn't do a pirouette—I got dizzy every time. All the other girls would do them, and when it was my turn I'd fall down. I failed her.

FRANCINE

It was a catalogue of failures, wasn't it?

EMILY

Oh, it was. I disappointed her so much. "Why can't you stand up straight? Why can't you do math? Why are you wearing that dress when it makes you look fat? Why don't you have a better job? Why don't you lose weight? Why don't you have a better house? A better husband? A better life?". It was endless.

FRANCINE
It was such negative energy, it was depressing. You wanted to be rid of it. It's why you moved so far away.

EMILY
Yes. Yes it was!

FRANCINE
And why you hardly ever came back.

EMILY
Yes, that's the reason. I couldn't take all the criticism, so I ran away. I left my mother when she needed me most. Oh, God, what a horrible person I am!

> *(Cries loudly. Francine offers a tissue for her to blow her nose. Emily blows her nose very noisily).*

Thank you.

FRANCINE
No problem. I always keep a supply with me. So, getting back to the subject.

EMILY
Yes.

FRANCINE
You're secretly glad she's not here.

EMILY
(Pause. Realization.) Oh my God, you're right! I've never admitted that, but it's true.

FRANCINE
You don't have her criticizing you anymore. Things have calmed down.

EMILY
Yes, yes they have.

FRANCINE
You are happier.

EMILY
I am happier, that's true.

FRANCINE
You are at peace.

EMILY
Yes, I am.

FRANCINE
You're ready to move on with your life.

EMILY
(Surprised). Yes, I think I am! I really think I am!

FRANCINE
Right! I think we're done here.

EMILY
Oh, thank you, this was really helpful. How much do I owe you?

FRANCINE
Fifty dollars cash. Sorry, I can't take plastic yet. Maybe next year.

EMILY
(Opens purse, pulls out some bills). Looks like I only have three twenties. Just keep the change, you're worth every penny. I feel so much better now!

FRANCINE
Thank you.

EMILY
Are you here every day?

FRANCINE

I'm open 365 days a year. If you want to see me on Mother's Day, though, you'll have to get on the waiting list. There's a huge backlog of guilt-ridden daughters I have to deal with.

EMILY

Well, I might be back. If I start to feel, you know…

FRANCINE

Guilty.

EMILY

Yes.

FRANCINE

Stop by anytime.

EMILY

Although I don't get out this way very much.

FRANCINE

I know. Minneapolis.

EMILY

But the next time I'm in town…

FRANCINE

Just look me up.

EMILY

Thanks.

FRANCINE

Don't mention it.

EMILY

Oh, and Merry Christmas!

FRANCINE

Same to you, dear. *(Turns and shouts)* Next!

Emily exits.

THE END

BAD HAIR DAY

CHARACTERS

LANCE   Around 40. Dressed in a suit and tie. Has a full head of neatly combed hair, but during the play his hair gets messier. At the end his coat is unbuttoned and his tie is askew.

LARRY   Somewhat older. Dressed casually. Overly friendly type.

ELLEN   Any age. An employee at the driver's license renewal center at the Department of Motor Vehicles. Dressed appropriate for work.

SETTING

An office at the Department of Motor Vehicles. Larry and Lance sit at chairs near Ellen's desk. They are sitting next to each other. Ellen is working at her computer.

TIME

Late afternoon, winter. The sun is setting outside.

At rise, Ellen is seated and Lance is standing in front of her desk.

LANCE

Excuse me, but will it be much longer before I can get my picture taken?

ELLEN

I told you before, we're running late today. We'll get to you when we can.

LANCE

Yes I know, but I really need to get that picture soon —

ELLEN

We'll get to you when we can, sir!

LANCE

Okay, I hope it's not much longer.

Sits down next to Larry

LARRY

Pretty impatient, aren't you?

LANCE
Well, I don't usually complain, but I've been waiting for a while.

LARRY
Getting your driver's license renewed?

LANCE
Yes, as a matter of fact, I am.

LARRY
Well, it'll take a while, buddy. What do you expect from the DMV? These people are slow as molasses.

LANCE
Yes, but I need to get it done soon, or —

LARRY
Because you're so important? Is that it? Look, you're no different than anybody else. We all have important lives, and we all have to wait when we come here. If you don't like it, you can leave.

LANCE
But I'm up against a big deadline. I really don't have much time. If I don't get this picture taken pretty soon —

LARRY

Well, you should have come in before the deadline. That's poor planning, my friend. You think you can just waltz in here and expect everything to stop for you because you waited so long to get your license renewed? What a narcissist.

LANCE

I'm not a narcissist, I just need to get this done right away. I have a very important reason.

LARRY

We all have an important reason—just keep your shirt on, will you? They'll get to you when they get to you. Actually, I'm pretty excited to get my picture taken. Usually I hate my driver's license picture, but today I'm thrilled. Want to know why?

LANCE

Well, no, I don't really—

LARRY

Because I had some work done. Yep, I finally joined the modern age and got some work done on my face. I resisted for years, but hey, you have to look your best today, right? I'm in sales, and I have to look good, it's my livelihood.

LANCE
Yes, I'm sure it is. Now if you'll just excuse—

LARRY
Want to know what I had done?

LANCE
Actually, no.

LARRY
Go ahead, take a look, I bet you won't be able to tell. It's very subtle, but it makes a difference.

LANCE
looks at him closely

I can't tell.

LARRY
It's my eyebrows.

LANCE
Your eyebrows?

LARRY
Yep! I used to have what's known as a unibrow. You know, looks like one big eyebrow that goes across my face? I was

always a little embarrassed by it. Well, this doctor I used—by the way, he got a five star rating on the Internet—got rid of it. Isn't it great? That's good work, wouldn't you say?

LANCE

I guess so. *(looks at his watch)* Oh no, it's really getting late. Excuse me. *(goes up to the counter again).* Pardon me, ma'am, do you think it will be soon?

ELLEN

I told you, we are having a busy day. We're short-handed, and we're very backed up.

LANCE

I understand that, but—

ELLEN

You'll have to be patient, please!

LANCE

Yes, but I have a time issue.

ELLEN

Don't we all? Please take a seat.

LANCE

Okay.

He sits down again

LARRY

I had to wait forever.

LANCE

puzzled

What?

LARRY

For my procedure. Had to wait so long to get
an appointment. But I did it, because I figure if
this doctor is so busy, he must be good, right?

LANCE

Right.

LARRY

It's a great thing, the way medicine has
advanced. Used to be, people like us, we were
finished. You get older, you get the wrinkles,
the hair growing in places it's not supposed to,
all those little flaws that pop up. You had to
accept it. Not anymore. Nowadays, you can
get yourself fixed up. Like you—you could use
a little work.

LANCE

What are you talking about?

LARRY

I hope you don't mind me saying, but you could use a little nip and tuck in the facial area. I mean, your face is fine, but it's a little long, with that prominent jaw. And you have the unibrow too, just like me. I'd definitely get that fixed.

LANCE

grits his teeth

Fixed?

LARRY

Oh, don't be embarrassed. It's just something we all need to do. By the way, it does wonders for your love life. Really perks you up, if you know what I mean.

LANCE

makes a throaty sound

Hmmph!

LARRY

Oh, you can scoff at it, but I'm telling you, you

get a little work done, you're going to feel like a new man.

LANCE
Makes a low barking sound, but tries to stifle it. Runs his hand through his hair, messing it up.

LARRY
Yep, you got it. You're going to feel like a new man, I'm telling you—you'll get that old predator attitude back. The leader of the pack!

LANCE
Growls a bit louder, still trying to stifle it. Runs his hand through his hair again, messing it up further.

LARRY
Ha, I get it. That old bedroom growl, huh? Yeah, that snarl that says I'm the top dog! That's the way you want to feel, buddy!

LANCE
Excuse me. *(goes to the counter again)* Uh, ma'am, I really, really need to get my picture taken, like right now. Please?

ELLEN

I've told you before —

LANCE

But *(stifles a growl)* you see, it's getting dark outside and —

ELLEN

I'm not going to tell you again — please take a seat!

LANCE

> *Goes back to his seat and emits a low,*
> *frustrated growl, then unbuttons his coat*
> *and loosens his tie.*

Grrr!

LARRY

I told you before, it does no good to get all worked up about this. Geez, look at you, buddy, you're all flushed, your hair is messed up. You're going to take a lousy picture now. Let me straighten your hair for you.

> *He reaches up to straighten Lance's hair,*
> *but Lance pushes his hand away.*

LANCE
Stop that! Rrrr!

LARRY
Okay, suit yourself—geez, I'm just trying to help. If you want to get your picture taken looking like that, fine, go ahead. But honestly, you could fix yourself up a bit. Boy, I didn't notice before, but you're really a hairy guy, aren't you?

LANCE
Growls again, bares his teeth

Rrrr!

LARRY
Geez, don't be so sensitive about your looks, buddy! It's nothing to be ashamed of. They can fix all that—the jaw, the big teeth, the hair. You'll feel like a new man, I'm telling you!

LANCE
Howls like a wolf.

LARRY
That's it! Get the old virility back! (*Howls himself*). That's the spirit, right? And man, you are quite the hairy specimen, aren't you?

Funny I didn't notice that before. It must be the light in here.

LANCE
Louder growl, showing more frustration. Runs his hand through his hair again, really messing it up this time.

LARRY
Yeah, I know it's frustrating—these government bureaucrats always make you wait. Just between you and me, I feel like ripping their lungs out sometimes. I mean, look out that window—we've been here so long it's getting dark outside. Oh, wait—is that a full moon coming up?

LANCE
Growls one more time, then panics and runs out.

ELLEN
watches him leave, then after a pause:

Next!

LARRY
calling after Lance

Hey, come back, I think it's your turn! Oh, well, it's probably for the best. He wouldn't have been happy with his picture anyway. Talk about having a bad hair day!

THE END

THE WORLD IS ENDING. AGAIN

CHARACTERS

ANDREA   Any age from 30-50.

BRIAN   Any age from 30-50.

JEN   Younger than them. In her twenties or early thirties.

SETTING

A coffee shop. At rise, Brian and Andrea are sitting at a table reading their cell phones.

TIME

Lunchtime, present.

Andrea and Brian are sitting at a table reading their cell phones when Andrea suddenly motions to him excitedly. They refer to their phones while they talk.

ANDREA

Oh my God, have you seen the news?

BRIAN

Yes, I just saw it.

ANDREA

It's terrible, isn't it?

BRIAN

It's like the world is coming to an end!

ANDREA

Definitely. It's definitely happening this time.

BRIAN

What will we do?

ANDREA

We should wait for the next news update, of course!

BRIAN

But shouldn't we do something?

ANDREA

No, there's nothing we can do.

BRIAN

Then we're doomed! Oh, wait, there's been an update. It's not as bad as we thought.

ANDREA

I see it. That's a relief.

BRIAN

Things are very bad, but the world is not ending.

ANDREA

That's good. I hate it when the world ends.

BRIAN

Do you remember last week?

ANDREA

You mean when the world was ending? Vaguely.

BRIAN

It was an apocalypse! But then it passed.

ANDREA

How did we survive? I'm not clear on the details.

BRIAN

I'm not really sure. Wait, I'm getting an update. Something new is happening!

ANDREA

Yes, I see it. Something really bad.

BRIAN

Really horribly bad.

ANDREA

Horrific. Just horrific!

BRIAN

It's worse than the last thing!

ANDREA

Much worse!

BRIAN

I feel a panic attack coming on with this one— that's always a good sign. Yep, it could happen with the next update.

ANDREA

Remember when the world wasn't ending all the time?

BRIAN

I can't remember that far back.

ANDREA

I think there was a time when the world didn't end quite as much. Maybe only once a month.

BRIAN

Once a month? Ha! You can't have anxiety when the world only ends once a month.

ANDREA

Right. And how can you live without anxiety? It's like oxygen for me.

BRIAN

It must have been like those tribes in the Amazon that have never experienced anxiety.

ANDREA

Really? There are tribes like that?

BRIAN

Scientists say there are people who have no fear of breaking news.

ANDREA

I can't imagine it.

BRIAN

What would we do if we weren't afraid all the time?

ANDREA

I know there are other emotions besides fear, but they're so boring.

BRIAN

How can you call yourself a human being if you don't have a bout of hysterical crying caused by naked fear once a day?

ANDREA

Or have to curl up in the fetal position with the covers pulled over your head every other day?

BOTH

It's the human condition, and we're fine with it!

ANDREA

looking at her phone again

Oh, here we go. Something's coming in now.

BRIAN
looks at his phone

What is it? I don't see it yet.

ANDREA
Oh, God. Oh, dear God.

BRIAN
What? What?

ANDREA
This is bad. This is really bad.

BRIAN
What is it? Wait, I'm getting an update. Oh, my, you're right.

ANDREA
Bad, right?

BRIAN
Terrible. Horrific.

ANDREA
It's definitely happening this time.

BRIAN
Yep. The world is definitely ending. Without a doubt.

ANDREA

This is too much. I don't know if I can take it this time. I'm thinking of turning my phone off.

BRIAN

And not get any updates? That would be stupid.

ANDREA

Oh, right. We need updates.

BRIAN

Otherwise, we wouldn't know how scared to be.

ANDREA

You're right. I would be lost without that feeling.

BRIAN

There's just no point in the world ending if we can't get updates that will terrify us.

ANDREA

Right. Oh, God, here's another one.

BRIAN

I just got one too. It's worse than I thought!

ANDREA

Much worse. Much worse than the last time the world ended!

BRIAN

Exponentially worse. This is really the big one!

ANDREA

Oh, God, the updates are getting worse and worse!

BRIAN

It's a chain of horrific updates! I've never seen anything like it!

ANDREA

Wait, the latest one is different.

BRIAN

Oh, right. Oh, it looks like it's not as bad as they predicted.

ANDREA

Yes. It looks like the crisis is over.

BRIAN

Wow, that was a close one!

ANDREA
Yeah, we really survived a close call.

BRIAN
We're survivors!

ANDREA
You bet. Survivors. We made it through another crisis!

BRIAN
Ain't no apocalypse here, baby!

ANDREA
You got that right!

Andrea looks at her phone with shock

BRIAN
Anything happening?

ANDREA
Omigod this is terrible!

BRIAN
What?

ANDREA
My phone just died.

BRIAN

Omigod, mine too!

ANDREA

All these updates must have drained the battery.

BRIAN

Mine too.

ANDREA

Now what are we going to do?

BRIAN

Yeah, we won't know if the world is ending now.

ANDREA

This is terrible.

BRIAN

Actually, it's kind of nice. Weird, but nice.

ANDREA

What do you mean?

BRIAN

It's so quiet. I think I hear the sound of birds chirping. Yes, I think it's birds chirping!

ANDREA

Is that what that is? I forgot what that sounded like.

BRIAN

And the breeze through the trees. That's kind of nice. Strange, but nice.

ANDREA

Wow. You're right, it is.

BRIAN

You think this some kind of alternate reality or something?

ANDREA

You mean a reality without news feeds?

BRIAN

Yeah.

ANDREA

I don't know. It's really weird, huh?

BRIAN

You bet.

ANDREA

But kind of nice.

BRIAN
Sort of. It's so quiet, though.

ANDREA
And my heart isn't racing anymore.

BRIAN
Me too. And I'm not sweating. I don't know how to handle this.

ANDREA
It's kind of peaceful, though.

BRIAN
Peaceful. I haven't heard that word in a while. What's it mean?

ANDREA
Quiet. Serene.

BRIAN
Yeah. Well, maybe this isn't so bad. (*beat*) I guess.

ANDREA
Right. Maybe we could get used to this.

BRIAN
To just exist, with no anxiety.

ANDREA

Right.

BRIAN

And no fear.

ANDREA

It would take some getting used to, of course.

BRIAN

But that would mean no updates forever, right?

ANDREA

Right.

BRIAN

I don't know if I can do it.

ANDREA

Maybe we should give it a try. It can't hurt us, right?

BRIAN

You sure? I mean, about the not hurting us?

ANDREA

What could happen? Let's try it.

BRIAN

Okay, if you say so.

They stare outward for a couple of beats, looking very bewildered.

Suddenly Jen rushes in

JEN

Run for your lives! The world is ending! This is the big one! It's really happening this time!

ANDREA

What's happening?

JEN

Don't you know? Haven't you looked at your news feeds?

BRIAN

Our phones are dead!

JEN

Are you kidding me? Listen, I don't have time to stand here and explain the situation to a couple of dummies who didn't keep their phones charged. Don't you realize you have to stay charged all the time? Otherwise you can't find out when the world is ending! What kind of people are you?

She starts to run off

ANDREA
Don't leave us! We need to get an update!

BRIAN
Can we borrow your phone?

JEN
Of course not—then I wouldn't know what's going on!

ANDREA
But what will we do?

BRIAN
We're really in a pickle now!

JEN
takes an extra phone out of her pocket and gives it to Andrea.

I don't know why I'm doing this, but here— it's my emergency phone. I always carry one in case my regular phone goes dead. You have to be prepared for everything in today's world!

ANDREA

Thank you so much!

BRIAN

We really appreciate this!

JEN

Don't mention it. Now if you'll excuse me, I have to go home and hide under the covers until the world ends.

ANDREA

Of course! Bye!

BRIAN

Bye!

JEN

Nice meeting you—while we're all still alive, I mean.

She runs out

ANDREA

Looks at phone

Oh, look, here we go. I see it—lots of information about the crisis!

BRIAN

Oh, good. I was starting to get worried there.

ANDREA

No, this is good. Really, really good. It's such a bad crisis. The worst!

BRIAN

sighs

I feel so much better now.

ANDREA

Oh, it's really bad. Probably the worst one in history.

BRIAN

Gee, that's great news.

ANDREA

I know! It's definitely happening this time. We should be scared out of our minds right now. Just primal, naked, screaming terror.

BRIAN

I'm so glad. It's so much better being terrified, isn't it?

ANDREA

I wouldn't have it any other way! *(Looks at the time on the phone)* Oh, wow, I didn't realize the time. I need to get back to work.

BRIAN

Me too! *(Gets up)* Gotta run. Have a great day!

ANDREA

You too!

BRIAN

See you here tomorrow?

ANDREA

Wouldn't miss it! Bye!

They exit in different directions.

THE END

JUST FIRE ME, PLEASE!

CHARACTERS

ASHTON PEPPER	A demon who is a regional sales manager in Hell. He appears to be 35.
CINDY KINDLE	A demon who works in the field, corrupting souls. She appears to be in her early 20s.

SETTING

An office in Hell. There is a desk and two chairs. Ashton Pepper is sitting at the desk, looking at a computer. Cindy Kindle enters, stage left.

TIME

Who knows? Somewhere in eternity.

CINDY

(Enters)

Hello? Mr. Pepper?

PEPPER

(Stands up)

Cindy Kindle! Come in, come in. So glad to see you.

CINDY

Yes, same here.

(They sit down)

PEPPER

I really appreciate you coming in on such short notice. I know you're busy.

CINDY

No, it's fine. It's an honor to be summoned for a meeting with you.

PEPPER

Good. I didn't take you away from anything

important, did I?

CINDY

Well, I have my normal backlog: a few crooked lawyers, a couple of teenage Satanists, some adulterers. Oh, and I have a heavy metal festival I'm signed up for. Things are heating up out there these days, as I'm sure you know!

PEPPER

Sorry to pull you away from that.

CINDY

Well, I can always pick up where I left off. Lawyers especially—they're already halfway to Hell when they come out of law school.

PEPPER

Good. Is there anything I can get you? Some blackened toast? A burnt hot dog? A cup of scalding hot coffee?

CINDY

No thanks, sir.

PEPPER

"Blackened toast," did you like that? (*chuckles*) Just my little joke. A little humor makes the eternity go faster, I always say.

CINDY

So, if we could just get down to business, Mr. Pepper? I've never been called in to the Regional Office before. I'm little wound up, as I'm sure you can imagine. I know the big sales meeting is next month, and I guess I'm in line for some type of award—

PEPPER

Ash—please call me Ash. No need to be nervous, Cindy, I'm sure we can get this straightened out in no time. So, actually, how are things out there in the field?

CINDY

Things are good! Very, very good, as I'm sure you can tell from my numbers!

PEPPER

Ha, ha, what a crazy gal, Cindy. You know we don't use that word, "good". We're all topsy turvy down here, you know that!

CINDY

Oh, of course. Things are bad. Really bad. Never worse, as a matter of fact.

PEPPER

That's the spirit, Cindy! But seriously, are you

getting results?

CINDY

Results? Why yes! Have you seen the latest quarterly numbers? I'm just killing it out there!

PEPPER

Uh huh. You want to tell me about those results, Cindy?

CINDY

Well, I thought you would know this already, but for starters, I'm responsible for, oh, about two dozen souls going straight to Hell. Just in the last quarter, that is. Doesn't that show up there in your spreadsheet?

PEPPER

Two dozen? That so? That's an impressive number.

CINDY

Well, thank you. I try to do a good—I mean a bad—job.

PEPPER

I bet you do. The thing is, Cindy, there does seem to be one little issue here. One tiny little problem.

CINDY

Oh? Like what?

PEPPER

Well, like the fact that none of those people has actually gone to Hell.

CINDY

They haven't? *(chuckles)* You must be looking at someone else's results. That's impossible!

PEPPER

No, I'm afraid it's very possible. And it's happened, Cindy.

CINDY

No, you must be getting me mixed up with someone else. My people all die with their souls in a state of total sin. No hope for redemption, those folks—they went straight to Hell.

PEPPER

You want to tell me how you know that?

CINDY

Well, I wasn't actually there when they died, of course. I was off corrupting more souls. That's what I do. I'm like the Soul Shredder, the Queen of Corruption, the Empress of Sin, the Baddest Bad Girl, the—

PEPPER

Right, right. Love those tags, Cindy, but can I be upfront with you? There's been some concern lately.

CINDY

Concern?

PEPPER

Yes. The folks downstairs—you know, way downstairs—are telling me that this is a pattern. Your clients are all repenting at the end.

CINDY

Repenting? No, that's wrong. None of my people would repent. I have them totally in my control. They're all complete sinners. Not possible.

PEPPER

But you weren't actually there when they breathed their last breath?

CINDY

Well. . . no, I wasn't.

PEPPER

Uh huh. I'm looking at a spreadsheet, Cindy, that says they all had a change of heart at the last minute.

CINDY

No way!

PEPPER

They repented of their sins. Wiped the slate clean. Hit the game-winning home run, if you will.

CINDY

You're sure about that?

PEPPER

It's all right here in the numbers. Is there anything you need to tell me, Cindy?

CINDY

pause

I don't know. Maybe?

PEPPER

Would you like to explain further?

CINDY

Well (*pause*) I guess so.

PEPPER

Mm-hmm?

CINDY

Oh, what the hell. I'm just not cut out for this. I mean, I try and all, but I just can't seem to get my head around the idea of eternal damnation. It's the "eternal" part that gets me. It's too final.

PEPPER

Final?

CINDY

Sure. I mean, eternal is a long time.

PEPPER

Tell me about it. However, rules are rules, Cindy, and we have to follow them, don't we? But, go on—is there something you still need to tell me?

CINDY

Well, sort of. I, uh—I guess you could say I give them a little, you know, wiggle room.

PEPPER

Wiggle room? What are you talking about?

CINDY

So, it's like this: when I get them to sign the contract where they sell their soul to me? I have an escape clause in it.

PEPPER

What exactly does that mean?

CINDY

Well, there's all this legal mumbo jumbo, but basically I have a clause that says, "If the corrupted one" — that's them, you know — "if the corrupted one decides at any time that he or she wishes to be forgiven, all he or she has to do is ask for said forgiveness from Upstairs, and this contract will become null and void." It's totally legal — I got a lawyer to write it all out in exchange for giving him a few tips on how to embezzle money from his client's firm.

PEPPER
(puts his head in his hands)

Cindy, what am I going to do with you?

CINDY

I know, it's a teeny bit unorthodox, right? We didn't learn any of that in sales training.

PEPPER

Unorthodox is hardly the word. I don't know where to start!

CINDY

See, I think about things, when I'm out there in the field causing mayhem in people's souls — taking over their bodies, making their eyes roll back in their heads, making them curse in Latin, making them vomit green bile, all that really gross stuff. Sometimes I get these crazy thoughts, you know?

PEPPER

Thinking is not good, Cindy. You're not supposed to think.

CINDY

Like, sometimes I think, what am I doing here? Why am I so bad?

PEPPER

You're a dark angel, Cindy. "Bad" is what we do.

CINDY

I should be embracing it, right? I should love the fact that I have all this power! But there are times when I'm just about to pull the trigger and get my clients to damn themselves for eternity, and wouldn't you know it, I get second thoughts.

PEPPER

Second thoughts? What kind of second thoughts?

CINDY

Like, what is the point here? Last week I got a call from some pimple faced boy who listened to too much heavy metal and thought he'd draw a pentagram and summon a demon, just for kicks. I mean, I wanted to say, "Dude, you're not even old enough to shave, and you're going to totally damn yourself for eternity?" Where's the justice in that?

PEPPER

Justice? Are you serious, Cindy?

CINDY

Well, I just thought that—

PEPPER

After what happened to us? Can you seriously talk about justice after what happened to us? After legions of us were banished?

CINDY

See, the thing about that is, I'm a little vague on the details. It was a long time ago, and I'm not sure I remember—

PEPPER

We were kicked out of Heaven, Cindy! Thrown into a bottomless lake of fire for eternity! We had the door slammed in our faces! We were banished, exiled, destroyed!

CINDY

Oh right, now I remember. Actually, I have a problem with that whole banishment thing. I feel like all I did was my God impression.

PEPPER

What are you talking about?

CINDY

Okay, picture this: I'm standing there with some of the other angels, just hanging out, you know, and we're all trying to make each other laugh. So, I do my God impression—that's the one where I use the deep voice and I'm all *(deep voice)* "Thou shalt not!" and "Thou shalt!" and I'm killing them, just killing, but then boom!—we're all hit with a thunderbolt, and I'm falling for what seems like months, and then I end up in Lava World here, which by the way, is really doing a number on my hair. I have to tell you, I think it was way over the line for God to punish me like that.

PEPPER

So, you don't like how things turned out. Is that right?

CINDY

Right. I think it was all a misunderstanding.

PEPPER

Are you serious?

CINDY

I don't really belong here, just for doing an impression, you know? Okay, maybe I don't have the voice down perfect, but still, this?

PEPPER

You think you were condemned to Hell for eternity because you did a bad impression of God? Is that what I'm hearing?

CINDY

Totally! It's just my wacky sense of humor, that's all! I don't think it's fair that—

PEPPER

breaks in

I'm glad you have a sense of humor, Cindy, but there's one thing you should be aware of — the people downstairs don't see anything funny in letting souls off the hook the way you're doing. Oh, they don't think that's funny at all. We're supposed to be helping every soul go straight to Hell. That's our *job*. It's your job, Cindy. You're not doing your job, are you?

CINDY

Well, technically, no.

PEPPER

So what are we going to do about this?

CINDY

I need a break.

PEPPER

What?

CINDY

I need a leave of absence. I'm totally burnt out. I need some time off.

PEPPER
You're burnt out? Did you just say you're burnt out? Was that a pun?

CINDY
I'm burnt out. I need a break.

PEPPER
What kind of nonsense are you talking here? There are no breaks in Hell, Cindy!

CINDY
I don't care, I need a break.

(Standing up)

I'm feeling like a little getaway to Antarctica. All those glaciers, the vast fields of snow, the intense cold. I have a soft spot for penguins, you know. They're cute little fellows.

PEPPER
"Cute"! What's the matter with you? We don't use words like "cute" here! Is this some kind of joke?

(Cindy starts to leave)

Cindy, where are you going? Come back here

this instant, or I'll—

CINDY
(Turns back)

Or you'll what? What are you going to do to me? Have you forgotten—I'M IN HELL ALREADY! THERE'S NOTHING YOU CAN DO TO ME! *(folds her arms)* Really, I want to hear this—tell me what you're going to do.

PEPPER
Don't try my patience, Cindy, I'm serious. Anything else out of you and I'm going to—

CINDY
You're going to what? Fire me? Are you going to fire me? Great! I'd love that, I really would. Go ahead, fire away!

PEPPER
This is insubordination! Disobedience!

CINDY
Yeah, well, I guess disobedience is something we're all familiar with down here, right?

PEPPER
Now you're being disrespectful! This is not good!

CINDY

Excuse me, we don't use that word, remember? You're supposed to say, "This is not bad."

PEPPER

You know exactly what I mean! Come back here, Cindy! Do you hear me? Come back here this minute! I'm warning you!

CINDY

Walking toward the door again

I'll be in touch. Yeah, I'll be in touch after I recharge the old batteries. A couple of months in Antarctica sounds good. I have a new comedy routine I want to try out on the penguins. And by the way, I want a transfer when I come back. I'm tired of the heavy metal scene. It's so late Eighties.

PEPPER

Damn you, Cindy! Come back here!

CINDY

But I'm already damned, remember? See you later!

She leaves

PEPPER
(Clenches his fists)

So, you need a break, huh? Well, we can fix that. *(Types on his computer)* There we go—a transfer to Washington, DC ought to do the trick. If you think eternity is long now, let's just see how long it feels when you're trying to get a politician to hold up his end of a deal!

THE END

WISH MY EGO WELL

CHARACTERS

ED BASCOMB	Sixty years old. Blustery, self-dramatizing. Wearing a windbreaker, jeans, and sneakers.
DORIS BASCOMB	She's been married to Ed for more than thirty years. Not as self-dramatizing as him, but smarter. Has a dry sense of humor. Also dressed for hiking, but carrying a camera bag. Accommodating, but with an edge to her.
MARY	Twenty five. Petite, very attractive. Wearing colorful spandex. Seems innocent, but has an edge to her also.

SETTING

The top of a mountain in Ireland. This is not a very high mountain. The stage represents a clearing at the top of the mountain. The set is minimal, just a small ring of stones, if possible, to represent a wishing well.

TIME

Afternoon, present time.

Doris and Ed appear from stage right. Doris is first. She gets excited when she sees the wishing well. She runs over to it and puts her camera bag down next to it. Ed comes after her and looks tired from the walk up the mountain.

DORIS
Look, there it is! The wishing well!

ED
That's it? That's what we climbed all the way up here for? If I knew you were going to make me climb Mount Everest on our vacation, I'd have agreed to your first idea, to go to Venice.

DORIS
This is Ireland, Ed. There's no Mt. Everest in this country. And you told me you'd never go to Venice. Besides, isn't it charming here? Just imagine how many people have made wishes in this well over the centuries!

ED
I bet it wasn't even here 20 years ago. It's just

an Irish scam to attract tourists.

                    DORIS
Why are you being so negative?

                    ED
You know I hate travel, Doris. We didn't have the money for this trip, anyway, not with what's happening in my business.

                    DORIS
It's my birthday present to you, Ed.

                    ED
Don't remind me about my birthday. I'm an old man, Doris.

                    DORIS
No, you're not!

                    ED
I'm a spent force. I'm a relic from the past. I'm a dinosaur.

                    DORIS
You're 60. That's not old!

                    ED
No, I'm finished. I've got nothing left to give.

I've lost my mojo.

DORIS

Ed, don't talk like that. Just because you've had a few setbacks.

ED

Setbacks? Is that what you call them?

DORIS

Yes, just little bumps in the road.

ED

Bumps in the road? Doris, have you seen the sales figures? I'm finished, done, kaput.

DORIS

Oh, I'm sure the sales will come back.

ED

For folding paper maps? Nobody buys them anymore, Doris. I'm in a business with no future. Even you, my own wife, you're using a GPS now. What's this world coming to?

DORIS

It's just easier, Ed. I don't get lost anymore. With the maps I was always getting lost.

ED

What's wrong with getting lost? People have been getting lost for centuries. Nobody was in such a hurry before, that's what the problem is. They didn't mind getting lost once in a while.

DORIS

It's just change, Ed.

ED

Well, I don't like change. I saw what it did to my father. "The Typewriter Eraser King" is what they called him. Look what happened to that poor man! A lifetime spent in the typewriter industry, and what did it get him? Nothing but a warehouse full of those little round erasers with the brushes on the end, and nobody to sell them to. And I'm headed down the same road!

DORIS

Ed, it's not that bad.

ED

Yes it is. I'm out of touch with the young people, too. I'm all thumbs when it comes to technology. I'm finished, Doris!

DORIS

Why don't we wish for something good to happen?

ED

What good will wishing do? That's not how the world works. It's a brutal, heartless world, and wishing won't change that.

DORIS

Oh, I bet it'll work. Otherwise, why would this well still be here after all these years?

ED

It's a scam, Doris. You don't get anything for free in this world.

DORIS

Ed, can we please enjoy this? Please?

ED

Oh, well, I guess it's worth a try. Let me find a coin. *(reaches in pocket).* Here you go. One for you and one for me.

DORIS

Pennies? Is that all you have? What about one of those Euro coins?

ED

Hey, those things are worth a dollar apiece in today's exchange rates. I'm not throwing one of them in there!

DORIS

Ed, you're being such a tightwad!

ED

Well, why won't a penny work? I don't see a sign that says, "No pennies please". The leprechauns aren't going to know the difference.

DORIS

Shh, you're not supposed to say their name! You say, "The Little People," remember? They told us that in the hotel. It's bad luck to say the "L" word.

ED

Oh, come on, Doris, will you stop? I don't believe in any of that stuff.

DORIS

Can't you spare a Euro or two? I read all the Irish legends before we came over, and they say The Little People are very miserly. The Little People will know the difference between a penny and a Euro.

                    ED
Yeah, well I'm one of the Big People, and we
don't waste our hard-earned cash.

                   DORIS
All right, I guess a penny will work. Can we
please make our wish now?

                    ED
Fine, go ahead. I'll play along with this silly
game.

                   DORIS
What are you going to wish for?

                    ED
I'm not telling.

                   DORIS
Oh, God, are you wishing for another woman?
A cute 25-year-old, right? That's what it is, isn't
it?

                    ED
Doris, what's the matter with you? I'm an old
man!

DORIS

I bet that's exactly what you're wishing for.

ED

You're wrong. Oh, sure it would be nice to see a 25-year-old woman with a big, er, smile come bouncing through the trees, but it wouldn't lift my spirits one bit.

DORIS

You're really a Gloomy Gus today, aren't you? Let's just do this, okay?

ED

All right, whatever.

DORIS

Here goes. We throw our coins in the well.

(They throw their coins in.)

DORIS

Now we close our eyes and make a wish.

(They close their eyes for two beats.)

DORIS

And that's it!

ED

That was a waste. I don't notice anything different.

DORIS

Maybe it takes a little while.

ED

Doris, I'm sorry to disappoint you, but you can't get what you want this easily.

DORIS

Well, it was worth a try.

MARY
(Enters stage right)

Hello? I didn't know anyone was up here.

ED
(stunned, takes a step backward)

My God!

DORIS

Hello, dear. My name is Doris. The man with his mouth open is my husband Ed.

MARY

My name is Mary. I'm from Cleveland. I'm here with my girlfriends, but nobody else wanted to walk up the mountain. Is this the well?

DORIS

Yes it is.

MARY

The Wishing Well?

ED

Yes, and it works! By God, don't let anybody tell you it doesn't!

MARY

Really?

ED

It's amazing. You just throw a coin in there, and your wish comes true!

MARY

How do you know that?

ED

Well, you see, it's the damnedest thing —

DORIS

I've never been to Cleveland, Mary. What's it

like?

MARY

It's nice, but not much happens there. That's why I came to Ireland, to add excitement to my life.

ED

Is that so?

DORIS

I know that feeling. You just want a little fun, a little romance, right? You want that tingly feeling you had in the past. You want—

ED

Don't put words in her mouth, Doris. She can speak for herself, she's not a child. No sir, she's a young, healthy, gorgeous—

DORIS

I'm not putting words in her mouth, Ed.

MARY

It's true, though. I want more out of life!

ED

I agree with you, Mary.

MARY

You do?

ED

(to Doris)

Yes, we all want more out of life, don't we dear?

DORIS

What? I must have a hearing problem, because I thought you said —

ED

Live for the moment! Go for the gusto, that's what I say!

MARY

You look like a man who's had a lot of exciting experiences.

ED

You bet! I'm always up for something new and exciting. I'm a risk taker, Mary!

DORIS

(testily)

Yes, he loves flirting with disaster, that one.

MARY

It would be nice if we could all be like you, Ed.
I mean, take me.

ED

Yes, let's take you, for example.

MARY

I sit at my desk and work with spreadsheets.
It's just numbers, numbers, numbers, all day
long. Sometimes I look out the window and
wonder what it would be like to just quit my
job and travel the world, you know?

ED

Why not do it?

MARY

Because I wasn't raised that way. I couldn't
just be a bum with no money. Money makes
the world go round, doesn't it?

ED

Money is overrated. It doesn't buy happiness, I
always say.

MARY

Well, I couldn't live without money. That's

why I couldn't quit my job.

                    ED
        (flirting)

You just need someone to show you around, Mary. A man with the wisdom of experience, but a devil-may-care attitude. A handsome, rakish, man of the world type who can help you enjoy your life. That's the ticket! You never know where you might meet somebody like that, Mary!

                   MARY
What wonderful advice!

                   DORIS
Oh, he's full of it.

                   MARY
You're so smart, Ed. You remind me of my grandfather, actually. He's such a throwback — he can't figure out how to use the GPS on his phone! People from your generation are so funny!

                    ED
        (deflated)

Right. Well, I'm always happy to help young people map out their lives.

DORIS
Ed's known as The Map King.

ED
(*gloomily*)

Sometimes you get lost, though.

MARY
Still, you make a good point.

ED
(*recovering his spirits*)

I know I do. In fact, I'll show you what I mean. Doris?

DORIS
Yes?

ED
Let's go to Venice!

DORIS
Venice? Really?

ED

Yes. You've always wanted to go there, haven't you?

DORIS
Yes, but you don't like to travel. You always say there's nothing worth seeing that's worth all the aggravation it takes to get there. You always say—

ED
I know what I always say, Doris, but forget that. I want to go to Venice and ride in a gondola and have a gondolier sing romantic songs to us in the moonlight!

DORIS
Ed, are you feeling okay? Is the air up here too thin for you?

ED
I'm feeling fine—never felt better in my life!

MARY
I've heard Venice is the dreamiest place.

ED
You hear that, Doris? Mary's heard it's the dreamiest place. I know—why don't we extend our vacation? We could add another

week in Venice.

DORIS

But what about the expense? You never want to spend your money on—

ED

Forget that. Money's no good if you don't use it. We need to cut loose, Doris!

DORIS

Well, I guess we could do it.

ED

Of course we could! We'll go back to the hotel and make our plans right now!

DORIS

All right.

ED

Good! Mary, it was nice to meet you. I recommend making a wish. It just might come true. Life is full of surprises!

MARY

Thank you, Ed. I will make a wish.

ED

That's the spirit, Mary. Now, we'll be off! We have plans to make. Goodbye!

MARY

Goodbye Ed, goodbye Doris!

(They exit.)

DORIS

(From offstage) Oh, darn, Ed, I forgot my camera bag. I'll go back and get it, you go on ahead. I'll catch up!

(Doris comes back and takes her wallet out).

So, how much do I owe you?

MARY
(with an Irish accent)

That'll be fifty Euros, madam.

DORIS
(counts out the money)

Okay, here you go. That was a great Cleveland accent, by the way.

MARY

'Tis a good teacher I have in drama school, Doris. He's done a bit of work with Meryl Streep, you know. Anyway, the pleasure was all mine, to be sure. 'Tis happy I am you got what you wanted.

DORIS
Oh, I did! I hope you did also.

MARY
Indeed I did! It was a fine bargain all around.

DORIS
Well, whatever it takes to get your wish, honey, that's what I say. Bye!

(exits)

MARY
Bye!

THE END

SECRET RECIPE

CHARACTERS

FRED KIBBLEHOUSE	Late 50s. A bit pompous. Dressed casually, and wearing an apron.
BRAD	Mid to late 20s. Dressed casually. Polite, but with a cocky edge.

SETTING

A patio or deck at a suburban home. There is a grill and a small table next to it. Fred is grilling hamburgers while Brad observes.

TIME

Late afternoon or early evening.

Fred Kibblehouse is standing at the grill, and Brad enters.

BRAD

Hello Mr. Kibblehouse.

FRED KIBBLEHOUSE

Hello Brad, good to see you.

BRAD

Mrs. Kibblehouse sent me out here to help you with the grilling.

FRED KIBBLEHOUSE

Yes, yes, I told her to. I thought you might want to come out, get an introduction to my grilling technique. Seeing as how you're coming in to the family and all.

BRAD

Oh, I'm happy to help, sir.

FRED KIBBLEHOUSE

Good man, Brad. Hand me that spatula, will you?

BRAD

Coming right up. Here you are.

FRED KIBBLEHOUSE

Thanks. Now, take those hamburgers out of the bags where they're marinating and put them on that plate.

BRAD

Wow, I didn't know you marinated your hamburgers.

FRED KIBBLEHOUSE

It's a special recipe. Passed down from my great-great grandfather. Believe me, I've had lots of people who want to know the ingredients, but my Dad swore me to secrecy, and I'll never tell.

BRAD

A secret family recipe. That's so cool.

FRED KIBBLEHOUSE

Yes, it's like Coca Cola. Did you ever hear the story about that?

BRAD

Coke? No.

FRED KIBBLEHOUSE

They guard that recipe like it's a secret weapon. Only three people in the world know the recipe, and they're all sworn to secrecy. If anybody ever reveals it, they have to be killed.

BRAD

Wow. Killed over a soda recipe. That's amazing.

FRED KIBBLEHOUSE

It's what's made Coke the market leader for so long. It's a symbol of America—known worldwide!

BRAD

So your recipe is like that?

FRED KIBBLEHOUSE

Well nobody's been killed—so far, ha ha—but if the recipe ever got out, we might have to consider it. It's that important to this family. My wife doesn't even know it.

BRAD

Mrs. Kibblehouse? She doesn't know the recipe? Why not?

FRED KIBBLEHOUSE

It's only passed down through the men in the family.

BRAD

I see. Do you have any other recipes like that? How about a marinade for hot dogs?

FRED KIBBLEHOUSE

No, son. One marinade recipe is enough. Besides, a hot dog is a hot dog is a hot dog. You can't do much with them. No, it's the hamburgers that really define this family, set us apart, if you will. You know, I only use the special recipe on big occasions.

BRAD

Really?

FRED KIBBLEHOUSE

Yes, and I'd say this is a big occasion, wouldn't you? The day my only daughter gets engaged?

BRAD

Oh yes! I'm very honored you chose the day when we got engaged to use your special recipe, sir. It really makes me feel like a part of the family.

FRED KIBBLEHOUSE

Oh, you're not part of the family yet, son. You're just engaged. Why, I hardly even know you! I mean, I only met you once before today, isn't that right?

BRAD

I know we haven't been going out very long, Mr. Kibblehouse, but—

FRED KIBBLEHOUSE

What is it—three months? That's the blink of an eye, my boy! But I know Angie's a very stubborn girl, and when she decides on something, well, her own father couldn't talk her out of it. No, it doesn't matter how much Daddy paid for her private education, dance lessons, music lessons, the trips to Europe to find herself—when it comes time to making a life-changing decision like getting married, well, good old Dad's supposed to just shut up and stay in the background. But, hey, the Kibblehouse's are nothing if not accepting. We welcome you with open arms, Brad!

BRAD

Thank you. That means a lot to me.

FRED KIBBLEHOUSE

And when my baby daughter, my only child, the apple of my eye, the sunshine of my life, the jewel of my existence gets engaged, that's a big enough deal to bring out the special marinade.

BRAD

I'm very honored.

FRED KIBBLEHOUSE

But, like I said, just being welcomed into the family doesn't mean I'll give you the special recipe. It'll take years before I can trust you enough to do that. I have to make sure the marriage will last.

BRAD

Oh, of course.

FRED KIBBLEHOUSE

I have no sons, and when a young man marries my daughter he has to prove himself for many years before I let him in on the secret. You'll be part of an exclusive club, more exclusive than any club on this planet. You will be sworn to secrecy, and you must keep the secret or you will suffer greatly for your transgression!

127

BRAD

Oh, don't worry about me, Mr. Kibblehouse. Mum's the word.

FRED KIBBLEHOUSE

Now hand me those hamburgers, will you? It's time to put them on the top rack. Hamburgers can burn easily, so I time them with military precision.

BRAD

Right. Here you go.

FRED KIBBLEHOUSE

Good. What do you think of that smell, huh? The marinade really comes out when the hamburgers cook. It's a mysterious, indescribable smell, don't you think?

BRAD

Actually, I'd say it smells like a blend of bourbon, brown sugar, a bit of pepper, and what's that other ingredient? Vanilla? Yes, that's it—a dash of vanilla. Although it's not the imported kind from Madagascar—no, that's definitely a cheap synthetic substitute.

FRED KIBBLEHOUSE

You recognized vanilla in there? There's only a

tiny—how did you do that?

BRAD

Oh I'd know that smell anywhere.

FRED KIBBLEHOUSE

I see. But how is it you're so—um, accurate—
at identifying a recipe by its smell?

BRAD

Oh, I've always been a foodie. I have an uncle
who's a five star chef in France, and I spent
every summer as a kid helping out in his
kitchen. I developed into a very good chef
myself. My uncle wanted me to join him as a
sous chef, but I declined, actually.

FRED KIBBLEHOUSE

But I thought you were an accountant!

BRAD

I am, but food is my hobby. The restaurant
field is very unpredictable, so I wouldn't make
it my career. I got an accounting degree just to
make sure I have a stable income.

FRED KIBBLEHOUSE

Yes, good idea. Very practical, son.

BRAD

That's just the first step, though. I'm going to law school next. I already got into Stanford, and I'll be starting there next Fall, after Angie and I get married. We'll be moving out to the coast, of course.

FRED KIBBLEHOUSE

But Angie has a good job here in Boston.

BRAD

Yes, she'll be leaving it at the end of the summer.

FRED KIBBLEHOUSE

You couldn't have gone to a law school around here?

BRAD

Oh, no. See, I want to do technology law, and Stanford's the best place for that. Close to Silicon Valley, of course.

FRED KIBBLEHOUSE

Of course.

BRAD

I have buddies who are already out there doing startups. That's my plan too—I have my career all mapped out. But you have to be out there to really use that talent pool — it's where the smartest people live.

FRED KIBBLEHOUSE
Right. So, that means you'll be out on the coast for quite a while?

BRAD
Probably forever. Have you ever been there? It's a paradise.

FRED KIBBLEHOUSE
California? No, I don't really like the culture there. Everybody's so pretentious. Really insufferable, actually. I don't know why they think they're so special — the schools out there are terrible.

BRAD
Ha, ha, that sounds just like someone from the East! People out here are such know-it-alls. They have that intellectual snobbishness, like there are no smart people outside of their little bubble. So parochial!

FRED KIBBLEHOUSE
Parochial? We do have all the Ivies in the East. If you want to call that parochial —

BRAD

chuckling

That's such an old school point of view. No, the action is in California. That's where all the smartest tech people are. Boston's just a backwater when it comes to tech. You have to be in Cali, and that's where Angie and I want to be.

FRED KIBBLEHOUSE

So, even when and if you have kids—

BRAD

Kids? Oh, no, we don't want kids. We're not into that.

FRED KIBBLEHOUSE

No kids?

BRAD

slaps him on the back

I bet you were hoping for some grandkids, right? Sorry about that, Dad, not going to happen.

FRED KIBBLEHOUSE

gritting his teeth

Yes, well, that's just the way your generation is, ha ha! No commitments, right?

BRAD

Yeah, we're all about personal growth. Kids get in the way of that. It's the same thing with marriage. I don't see any reason why we have to remain faithful to each other in our marriage. That's just an old-fashioned, East Coast way of looking at things. No, monogamy is just a straitjacket, really.

FRED KIBBLEHOUSE

Straitjacket? I see. Well, I guess you young people need your freedom, right? No obligations to family, tradition, roots? The past means nothing, I guess!

BRAD

So, it looks like those burgers are about ready. Want me to try one, just to see?

FRED KIBBLEHOUSE

Oh, yes. Now, this is a big moment, Brad, when you get to taste the marinade for the first time. Savor it slowly, okay? There you go.

Hands a burger to Brad

                    BRAD
Thanks.

              He takes a bite
            FRED KIBBLEHOUSE
Well, son, what do you think?

                    BRAD
              spits it out

Terrible!

            FRED KIBBLEHOUSE
Terrible?

                    BRAD
That was disgusting! I wouldn't feed that to a
dog. My uncle would be appalled.

            FRED KIBBLEHOUSE
But—

                    BRAD
Those ingredients don't mix well at all! Do
you have anything I can rinse my mouth out
with?

            FRED KIBBLEHOUSE
Rinse your mouth out? Why?

                    134

BRAD

I need to get rid of this horrible taste!

FRED KIBBLEHOUSE

But people love that marinade! Many, many people have asked for the recip—

BRAD

It goes to show that you have underdeveloped palates on the East Coast. God, this is really bad stuff!

FRED KIBBLEHOUSE

You think so, huh?

BRAD

I have to get this taste out of my mouth! Do you have anything to drink out here?

FRED KIBBLEHOUSE
getting an idea

No. But I think I can remedy the situation. Just wait here. And watch those burgers—I don't want them to burn.

BRAD

Okay, but hurry up, will you? I'm dying here.

FRED KIBBLEHOUSE
I'll be back in no time.

*Exits, then comes back a moment later
with a glass of water*

Okay, I'm back. Here you go, son. Take a nice big drink of that.

BRAD
Thanks.

gulps it down

FRED KIBBLEHOUSE
Feel better?

BRAD
Yes. I couldn't stand that taste one second longer. Sorry, I mean I know it's your special recipe and all, but, I guess my palate is just too sophisticated. I mean, that stuff was really bad. Like, world class bad!

FRED KIBBLEHOUSE
Well, to each his own.

BRAD
I hope I didn't swallow any of that hamburger.

I'm getting the weirdest feelings in my stomach.

FRED KIBBLEHOUSE
Oh, I don't think you swallowed it. I saw you spit it all out.

BRAD
I don't know. I'm really not feeling well all of a sudden.

FRED KIBBLEHOUSE
That's too bad.

BRAD
You don't think it was the water, do you? Is that well water? I don't like drinking well water.

FRED KIBBLEHOUSE
No, it's our public water. Of course, it's just Massachusetts water. Nothing like you'd get in California I'm sure, but it does the trick for us. Once in awhile I add a little something to it, but I'm sure that's not the problem.

BRAD
I don't know what's come over me. I need to sit down.

FRED KIBBLEHOUSE
Go right ahead. I'll take care of the burgers.

BRAD

gasping

Getting hard to breathe. It's weird, I think my throat is closing up. And I'm sweating to death here.

FRED KIBBLEHOUSE
Oh, you're probably just imagining—

BRAD
No, it's true. What's the matter with me? What did you mean by "add a little something" to the water?

FRED KIBBLEHOUSE
Oh, nothing, really—well, I might have put in a drop of something to improve the effect.

BRAD
The effect? It's water! Water doesn't have an effect! What did you put in it? I'm really not feeling good at all.

FRED KIBBLEHOUSE
Oh, just a little something for my future son-

in-law. Something with a little kick to it.

BRAD
gasping more

Can't catch my breath. Call 911, call 911!

FRED KIBBLEHOUSE
looking around

Oh, damn, I can't seem to find my phone. Where did I put it?

BRAD
Never mind, I'll do it. (*Takes out his phone*). Oh, God, my vision's getting blurry! I can't see the screen.

FRED KIBBLEHOUSE
They make those screens so hard to read these days. I don't know who designs those things, but—

BRAD
Go inside and tell Angie!

FRED KIBBLEHOUSE
But I can't leave these burgers, son. They're almost done, and if I leave now they'll burn. I

would never serve my guests burnt hamburgers. It's just not done here in Boston.

BRAD
Mr. Kibblehouse, I'm begging you!

FRED KIBBLEHOUSE
I'm sure you'll feel better in a minute. It's just a little gas, probably.

BRAD
It's not gas! I'm, uh, oh no *(slumps over)*

FRED KIBBLEHOUSE
Goes back to flipping burgers

Oh well, I guess you'll never get to learn the secret recipe. What a pity—and I forgot to tell you about the other secret recipe we have, son. Of course, that one doesn't have much of a taste to it—cyanide never does.

THE END

PEP TALK MAN TO THE RESCUE!

CHARACTERS

RALPH About 30. He's depressed and anxious about his life, and he's thinking of ending it all. Dressed in jeans or sweatpants and a t-shirt.

PEP
TALK
MAN About 40. Full of enthusiasm. He is dressed in colorful boxer shorts and an undershirt, plus white socks.

SETTING

Ralph's bedroom in his apartment. It is furnished very sparsely. The main furniture is a bed, and Ralph is lying in the bed when the play starts. There is also a chair at the foot of the bed.

TIME

Late afternoon. Present.

AT RISE

Ralph is in bed.

RALPH
This is the end. There's no use. I just can't do it anymore.

PEP TALK MAN
enters, stage right, leaping into the room

Stop! Don't make any rash decisions!

RALPH
What? Who are you? What are you doing in my room?

PEP TALK MAN
I'm Pep Talk Man!

RALPH
Pep Talk Man? Are you some kind of a nut? How did you get in here?

PEP TALK MAN

No, I'm not a nut, and I got in here because in your weakened mental state you left the front door unlocked. With my superpowers I detected the signs of depression, and I went into action!

RALPH

agitated

But you're in your underwear!

PEP TALK MAN

This is a crisis, young man! I came as fast as I could, there was no time to worry about clothing.

RALPH

This can't be real. I must be dreaming.

PEP TALK MAN

No, you're not dreaming. Let me explain: I have a special superpower that tells me when someone is depressed. You know how some people get a pain in their big toe when it's going to rain? Well, I'm like that with depression. I feel that moist negative energy in the air and pow! I race to the scene.

RALPH

Are you a burglar? You must be a burglar. Or maybe you're a serial killer. Oh, God, are you a serial killer?

PEP TALK MAN

I'm not a burglar, and the only killing I do is to nuke the blues! You like that? "Nuke the blues". I think I'm going to make it my new catchphrase.

RALPH

This is surreal. I should call the police, but what's the use? I'm too depressed to pick up the phone.

PEP TALK MAN

See! That's why I'm here!

RALPH

I must be hallucinating you. That's it—you're a hallucination.

PEP TALK MAN

I'm no hallucination! I'm as real as your depression, son!

RALPH

Then my mind is playing tricks on me.

PEP TALK MAN

Exactly! Here's how it works: your mind is a supervillain who wants to take over your universe, and you need help to fight him off! I know all his ploys, all his tricks, and I can help you defeat him!

RALPH

No, you can't help. I'm thinking of ending it all.

PEP TALK MAN

That's your mind talking.

RALPH

Well of course it is. I don't see anyone else in the room who's telling me to kill myself. It has to be my mind.

PEP TALK MAN

Your mind is EVIL!

RALPH

You keep saying that.

PEP TALK MAN

Because I know my stuff. I've been doing this for years, you know.

RALPH

Really?

PEP TALK MAN
sits on the edge of the bed, crosses his legs

Let me tell you the backstory. I was a lonely little orphan boy who developed a bad case of teenage depression. I was experimenting with some radioactive materials in my basement, trying to find a cure for my acne, when I decided to take a drink of the mixture, just to see how it would taste (I know, stupid thing to do, but isn't that always the way with young superheroes?). So I drank the formula and pow! I became Pep Talk Man! The scourge of depression everywhere!

RALPH
I don't believe in superheroes.

PEP TALK MAN
You're looking at one right now! Pep Talk Man! In the flesh!

RALPH
Shouldn't you have a cape? And a costume? I thought superheroes wore costumes.

PEP TALK MAN

It's at the cleaners. I've been meaning to get another one made, but I've been so busy. You wouldn't believe how many depressed people there are! I have a waiting list as long as my arm. Actually, I've been thinking of getting a sidekick to help me with this backlog. I like the name Cheerful Boy. What do you think? Has a ring to it, doesn't it?

RALPH
puts his head in his hands

This conversation is getting weirder by the minute.

PEP TALK MAN
laughs

No, there's absolutely nothing weird about me being in your bedroom in my underwear. Nothing at all, trust me.

RALPH
Are you some new kind of psychiatrist? I bet that's it!

PEP TALK MAN
Nope. Actually, psychiatrists hate me. They're

suspicious of someone who just flies in and defeats depression in one visit. I'll tell you, though, the insurance companies love me!

RALPH
I'm sure they do.

PEP TALK MAN
Look, here's one of the things your mind does. It sees everything in black and white terms. There's no middle ground. You're either a roaring success or an utter failure. So, since most of us can find plenty of areas where we didn't perform up to our unrealistic standards, it's easy to focus on the failures.

RALPH
You're right about that. I'm a complete failure in every part of my life.

PEP TALK MAN
But that's the problem, my mixed up friend! You're too preoccupied with the failures. Let's take a look at your life, and I'll show you. What's your career situation?

RALPH
I'm a writer.

PEP TALK MAN

A writer? No problem, I deal with a lot of your kind. Now, exactly why do you think you're a failure?

RALPH

Because my books don't sell.

PEP TALK MAN

Uh, huh. Look, just because you're not on the best-seller list, that doesn't mean —

RALPH

I don't sell anything. Nada. Zero. Zilch. My sales are so bad my publisher and agent both dropped me.

PEP TALK MAN

Well, what are your books about?

RALPH

The hopelessness of modern life. See, I've given this a lot of thought, and —

PEP TALK MAN

Okay, next question. Got any family?

RALPH

No family. They were all killed by a tsunami in

my hometown. You know, it's unusual to have tsunamis in Wisconsin, but that day—

PEP TALK MAN
Got it. Let's move on to relationships. Tell me, do you have a special someone? Someone you love?

RALPH
I haven't had a relationship in years. I have a hard time connecting with women.

PEP TALK MAN
How about men?

RALPH
Them too.

PEP TALK MAN
I don't suppose you have a pet?

RALPH
I had a fish once, but it died.

PEP TALK MAN
It figures *(sighs).* This is a hard case.

RALPH
I told you. You won't be able to help me, I guarantee it.

PEP TALK MAN
Yes. *(Beat)*. Well, it won't be the first time.

RALPH
What do you mean?

PEP TALK MAN
I don't have a 100 percent success rate.

RALPH
Oh? What is your success rate, if you don't mind me asking?

PEP TALK MAN
That's a secret. Superheroes don't talk about things like that.

RALPH
Well, is it 75 percent?

PEP TALK MAN
It's a secret, I said! Let's just say it's less than 75 percent.

RALPH
How about fifty percent? Do you cure half the people you deal with?

PEP TALK MAN
Less.

RALPH
Really? What about 25 percent? That's one in four.

PEP TALK MAN
I said I don't want to talk about it!

RALPH
But how can you call yourself a superhero? How can you call yourself Pep Talk Man when you don't help anyone who's depressed?

PEP TALK MAN
(Beat). It's all a big lie. I'm a phony, a fraud. My life is a failure. I can't help anybody!

puts head in hands and sobs

RALPH
Aw, it can't be that bad.

PEP TALK MAN
No, it is! It's terrible. I can't go on living this lie.

RALPH

You must be helping someone. Come on, tell me the last person you helped.

PEP TALK MAN

Well, I sort of helped this high school kid who got dumped by his girlfriend and was feeling blue.

RALPH

See! You did help someone!

PEP TALK MAN

He ended up shooting holes in her car.

RALPH

Oh. Well, that's something. I mean, at least he took some action. He dealt with his feelings.

PEP TALK MAN

He's in jail now.

RALPH

I see.

PEP TALK MAN

Listen, can I get in your bed? I'm feeling really bad. I don't think I can go on.

RALPH
Okay, sure.

They change places. Pep Talk Man gets into the bed, and Ralph sits in the chair.

PEP TALK MAN
My life sucks.

RALPH
No, you're just having a bad day. It happens to all of us.

PEP TALK MAN
Superheroes aren't supposed to have bad days. They're supposed to be invincible.

RALPH
That's the kind of thinking that gets you in trouble. Nobody's perfect. It's when we try to meet these impossible standards, that's when we get depressed. Believe me, I know. I wanted to be Ernest Hemingway, and that was setting the bar way too high.

PEP TALK MAN
Hemingway? Didn't he kill himself?

RALPH

That's right! See, even he couldn't live up to the Ernest Hemingway standard. And if he couldn't do it, how could I? No, we have to accept ourselves with all our frailties, not try to be some superhuman version of ourselves.

PEP TALK MAN

You have a point there.

RALPH

Sure I do! I mean, look at you—running around all day long trying to be perfect, trying to save every depressed person in the world—it's impossible! Not even a superhero could do that.

PEP TALK MAN

You don't know how hard it's been to live up to my image. People have so many problems! I can't solve them all. I've just been kidding myself that I could do it.

RALPH

Absolutely. Come on, go easy on yourself. You're allowed to fail once in awhile. In fact, you can fail a lot. It's all part of life.

PEP TALK MAN

Thanks. I needed to hear that.

RALPH

Don't mention it.

PEP TALK MAN

You know, I feel a lot better. I think I can go on now.

He gets out of the bed

RALPH

Great! I'm happy for you.

PEP TALK MAN

Hey, you're pretty good at this. You should consider going into one of the mental health professions.

RALPH

You think so?

PEP TALK MAN

I know so. You have a gift. And you know what? I think you'd make a great Cheerful Boy.

RALPH

Me?

PEP TALK MAN

You'd kill out there, I guarantee it. We'd be a

great team! And by the way, I know a guy who's a whiz at designing superhero costumes. I see you in canary yellow, with red trim and a kelly green cape. It would bring out your eyes.

RALPH
I don't know, I might feel silly.

PEP TALK MAN
laughs

My clients are so depressed they hardly even notice the costume, believe me. But anyway, think about it. Here's my card. If you change your mind, give me a call.

He hands his business card to Ralph

RALPH
All right, I will.

PEP TALK MAN
Well, I have to be going.

RALPH
Me too. I think I'll go out and get some coffee and a bite to eat. Maybe I'll do a Google search, look up the requirements for a career in counseling.

PEP TALK MAN

That's the spirit! Well, listen, this has been great, but I have to run.

RALPH

Sure. Stop back anytime.

PEP TALK MAN

I will, I will! But I don't think you'll be needing me for awhile.

RALPH

You think so? You may be right. I do feel like I've turned a corner here.

PEP TALK MAN

Great! Now I have to make my exit. A good exit is very important in the superhero game, you know.

RALPH

Right.

PEP TALK MAN

Here goes. "Another depression KOed, thanks to Pep Talk Man!"

He runs out of the room

FUNNY SHORTS

RALPH

What a guy!

THE END

RATING THE BREAKUP

CHARACTERS

MARK   Mid-twenties. Dressed in jeans and
           jacket.

AMY   Same age. Dressed in a casual but
           attractive style.

SANDY   Same age. Dressed a bit more casually,
NICOLE   in jeans.
           Same age. Also dressed in the same
           style.

SETTING

A coffee shop in the city. Amy is sitting at a table with her coffee. Sandy and Nicole are sitting nearby.

TIME

Late afternoon.

MARK

enters, embraces Amy. She does not get up.

I'm sorry I'm late.

AMY

It's okay.

He sits down, seems nervous.

AMY

What's the matter? You seem upset.

MARK

takes a deep breath

So Amy, I've been thinking about something.

AMY

Yes?

MARK

We've been going out for a while now.

AMY

Actually, it's been a year, Mark. This is our anniversary.

MARK

Right. A year. Well, what I was going to say is. . .

AMY

Yes?

MARK

I, uh, think we need to see other people.

AMY

What? Are you serious?

MARK

Yes. I've given it a lot of thought, and—

AMY

You've given it a lot of thought? How about involving me in this? So you just did all your thinking, and you came to this conclusion without talking to me?

MARK

I know this is hard, but—

AMY

I can't believe this.

MARK

We're just not suited for each other.

AMY

That's the stupidest breakup line I've ever heard.

MARK

We've grown apart.

AMY

And that's the second stupidest. You really aren't good at this. This is terrible. This isn't even a one star performance here.

MARK

What do you mean, one star?

AMY

Your review on Breakup.com. You're going to get a lousy review from me, Mark. This is a very poor showing.

SANDY

chimes in

I agree. I was thinking two stars at first

because he was nervous and I was going to give him a break, but no, this is definitely a one star performance.

NICOLE

Totally one star. In fact, I've already posted it. I just want to make sure—is your name Mark or Marcus?

SANDY

It's Marcus, right Amy?

AMY

Yes. Marcus Brown.

MARK

Wait, how do you two know my name?

AMY

You were late, I started talking to them. Just girls talking, that's all. But I had a feeling you were going to do this, so I told them to be ready to post a review.

SANDY

Typing on her phone

I'm posting mine now actually.

MARK

Review? What kind of review are you talking about?

AMY

A relationship review. I have to say, this performance is going to drop your rating quite a bit.

MARK

What do you mean?

AMY

Oh, come on, you can't seriously expect me to believe you don't know about relationship ratings, do you? I use Breakup.com, but there are half a dozen others out there.

MARK

Uh, no, I don't, I've never—

AMY

You didn't check my rating before we started going out?

MARK

No, I never heard of such a—you have a rating?

AMY

It's four stars. I'm quite a catch.

SANDY

She's right. I looked her up. Four stars.

NICOLE

Some great comments, too.

SANDY

I like this one: "She's velvety smooth at breaking up".

NICOLE

And this one: "I've never been dumped with such class before. She's the best!"

AMY

I'm proud of my breakup skills.

MARK

You mean people rate each other on their breakups?

AMY

Sure, why not? There are ratings for everything else. Why not for breakups?

SANDY

It's really a great thing.

NICOLE

Takes the unknown factor out of your relationships. You can check somebody's rating before you get involved with them — makes it much more efficient.

AMY

I checked your rating last year when we started going out. I have to tell you, it made me pause — three stars. I usually never go below four.

MARK

Three stars? I got three stars?

AMY

Yep. And there were comments that raised some concern.

SANDY

Oh yeah, I'm reading one now. "He broke up with me by text. What a jerk!" It's signed Allison.

MARK

Allison? My last girlfriend? That's not fair! I

did technically break up with her by text, but I called right after I sent the text. I just wanted to break the ice with a text, that's all. She's not being honest with that review!

AMY

Well, you're stuck with it, babe.

NICOLE

Yeah, she gave you two stars. It really tanked your rating.

AMY

Before that you were doing pretty good. You actually had a four star rating at one point a few years ago.

MARK

Well, that's probably from Sarah, my girlfriend in college. We both realized in senior year that we weren't compatible anymore, so it was easy. And, well, my only other relationship since then was Allison, so I haven't had much practice in breaking up.

SANDY

Practice makes perfect!

NICOLE

Right. You'll get better at this after a few more breakups.

AMY

It's a shame you're so inexperienced, but that's life. I can't worry about it—you'll have to pull your rating up with the next relationship, Mark. I'm out of here.

She stands up

MARK

Wait, does this mean I'll have a hard time meeting someone now?

AMY

Of course. People check ratings all the time. With my one star review, you're going to go through a long dry spell, I'm afraid. Nobody wants to go out with a dude who's so bad at breaking up.

SANDY

To Nicole

I wouldn't go out with a one star, would you?

NICOLE
No way. That's a big red flag for me.

MARK
Wait, wait! Is there anything I can do to get you to change my rating? Please?

AMY
Nope, you'll have to live with it.

SANDY
Yeah, that's just the way it is.

MARK
No, please! How about if I send flowers? Would that help? Or a poem! How about if I write a poem about our breakup?

AMY
I'm not that in to poetry, sorry. And I'm allergic to flowers, which you should know by now. The fact that you don't is another stain on your record, Mark. I might have to add that to my review.

MARK
A gift? How about a gift? Would that work?

AMY

It might, but it depends on what the gift is.

MARK

How about a bracelet?

AMY

Tacky.

MARK

A book?

AMY

I don't trust your taste in authors. I saw what you have in your bookcase. Westerns? I thought nobody read Westerns anymore. You're not a gun nut are you?

MARK

How about tickets to a concert?

AMY

What band?

MARK

Your choice, just give me the name and you've got a ticket.

AMY

Two tickets. I'm moving on, Mark. I'll be taking a date to the concert, and it won't be you.

MARK

You want me to buy a ticket for another guy? No way!

AMY

turns to walk away

Fine. I'll be leaving now.

MARK

Wait! Okay, two tickets.

AMY

Good. But I'm not giving you any more stars unless I get front row center seats. I'll text you some names of bands I like, and we'll see what you get me.

MARK

No problem! It's as good as done. Will you give me four stars if I get you really good seats?

AMY

Nope, that's asking too much. I'll take you up

to three, but that's it. I have standards to maintain. I don't want to get banned from the breakup sites.

SANDY

That would be bad news.

NICOLE

Oh, yeah, that's the kiss of death. Very hard to recover from that.

MARK

Okay, three stars will have to do. Thank you! Thank you very much! I really appreciate this!

AMY

Don't mention it. See you around, Mark.

She leaves

SANDY

You're really lucky, Mark.

NICOLE

Yeah, that could have done real damage to your love life.

SANDY

Could take years to get out of a mess like that.

NICOLE
Decades!

MARK
Wow, I do feel like I dodged a bullet there.

SANDY
I recommend you start a profile right now on Breakup.com.

NICOLE
It's never too soon!

MARK
You're right. I'm going to do that right now!

Gets out his phone

SANDY
No, first the tickets, Mark. Buy her the tickets.

NICOLE
Yeah, you need to get that rating changed ASAP.

MARK
Oh, right. The tickets! It's a small price to pay for a good rating!

Starts looking up tickets on his phone

SANDY
to Nicole, as they get up to leave

Technology is such a great thing, isn't it?

NICOLE
Honestly, I don't know how people ever had relationships in the past.

They leave, as Mark is frantically searching for tickets on his phone.

THE END

JUST SAY YES

CHARACTERS

HAROLD   In his 60s, blustery, emotional.

LOUISE   Harold's wife. Also in her 60s. Smart
            and practical-minded.

TOMMY   Their son. He's 35 and still living at
            home. He's smart but nerdy and a bit
SARAH   immature.

            Tommy's girlfriend. She is thirtyish,
            earnest and friendly.

SETTING

The living room of Harold and Louise's home. There is a couch and several chairs.

TIME

Evening, around 5:30.

*At rise Harold is pacing nervously
around their living room, while Louise
sits on the couch and watches him.*

LOUISE

Harold, what on earth is the matter, why are
you so anxious?

HAROLD

Oh, nothing. Everything is perfectly normal.
No problem at all. What time is it?

LOUISE

It's five minutes since the last time you asked
me that question. Harold, you can't fool me —
after 35 years of marriage, I know when you're
nervous. What is it?

HAROLD

sits down across from her

Okay, Louise, I'll be straight with you. I really
want things to go well tonight.

LOUISE

You mean with our anniversary dinner? That's

so sweet of you, to be anxious about giving me a perfect anniversary dinner.

HAROLD
Oh god, no, not that. I mean, uh, yes, I do want you to have a great anniversary dinner, of course. Of course! But there's more to it than that.

LOUISE
What could possibly be more than that?

HAROLD
I want this night to go well for Tommy.

LOUISE
Our son? What do you mean?

HAROLD
Look, this is a big night. He really loves this Sarah he's been dating, and he's close to proposing. That's why he asked to come to dinner with us—he's going to pop the question tonight! It's going to happen, Louise. After all these years, he's ready to get married! He's finally going to become an adult!

LOUISE
He's an adult already. He's 32 years old, if you remember.

HAROLD

Yes, he's 32 years old and still living at home. I didn't expect to have my kid living with me this long. It's time to kick him out of the nest, Louise!

LOUISE

He's still finding his way.

HAROLD

Finding his way? At his age I was halfway through adulthood. What's he got—a wall full of degrees, a job at the mini-mart, and a podcast about Star Trek. Is that what we paid all that tuition for—Star Trek? You know how we feel about Sarah, Louise—she's a winner. God, I'm hoping this works. This could be his last chance!

LOUISE

What do you mean? Any woman would be happy to marry him—when he's ready, of course.

HAROLD

Look, I don't care if he's ready or not, I want him out of here. There's just one problem: she's terrified of marriage. He told me her parents' relationship was a nightmare, and

185

now she's afraid of commitment. He's not sure she'll say yes if he proposes. And if she turns him down he'll probably spend the next two years moping in his bedroom. God, it makes me shudder to even think it!

LOUISE
Marriage isn't the only option. They can just live together. That's what all the millennials do anyway.

HAROLD
Not on your life! You know what'll happen — they'll live together for a few months and the magic will wear off and then we'll have him back. No sir, I want it all wrapped up legally and tied with a big fat bow. I want the whole nine yards — the priest, the ring, the ceremony. I want the official seal of approval.

LOUISE
That doesn't mean anything. They can always get a divorce.

HAROLD
I know that. But that's why we have to be on our best behavior tonight. These kids just need someone to show them the benefits of marriage. They need a good example, Louise —

like us. Look at us—35 years married and never a problem. We're a glowing example of marriage!

LOUISE

Yes, I suppose we are. Although I don't agree with the "never a problem" part.

HAROLD

Not tonight, Louise! No, no, no. For tonight we have no disagreements whatsoever. Got it? No disagreements about anything. I want us to show Sarah a marriage that really works!

LOUISE

But that's no fun. I like disagreeing with you.

HAROLD

Nope, not tonight! There are no nos tonight— everything is yes, yes, yes. Okay?

LOUISE

Oh, all right.

HAROLD

Good. It won't be long till they get here. We'll go to our favorite restaurant, and everything will be just perfect. We'll be charming and witty, and Sarah will get a good look at our successful marriage. After that Tommy can take her for an after dinner drink and propose, just like I advised him. Then it's on to the next step, Louise! We sell this house and downsize like we've been talking about for ages.

LOUISE

Like you've been talking about for ages. I never said I wanted to downsize.

HAROLD

But Louise, we don't need this big house. I'm sick of taking care of it. It's old and drafty, and the utility bills are too high. The taxes are outrageous, let's not forget that. And I'm tired of cutting the grass and shoveling the snow in the winter. I want out of here, Louise!

LOUISE

It's not just about you, Harold. I like this place. I like my garden, I like the big kitchen, and I like our neighbors. Oh, and by the way, I'm not ready to retire from teaching, and the university is only a 20 minute commute from here. Besides if we downsize I'll have to get rid of so many things.

HAROLD

Exactly! We need to get rid of the baggage in

our lives—including Tommy!

LOUISE

Our son is not baggage.

HAROLD

It's a metaphor, Louise. I'm just trying to say that it's time for me—for us—to get on with our lives. We've done the parenting thing. It's time for us to spread our wings, to travel. Don't you want to travel?

LOUISE

Yes I want to travel.

HAROLD

That's the spirit! We'll go hiking in the Rockies, camping in the wilds of Alaska, whitewater rafting on the Colorado River. Oh, and I've heard the Amazon rain forest is spectacular!

LOUISE

I don't like those kinds of trips. You know that.

HAROLD

I know, but we haven't done it the right way. I think you'd really like to go hiking in the—

LOUISE

I don't like hiking. I never liked hiking.

HAROLD

Yes, I know, but I thought maybe when we retired and we had the time—

LOUISE

What made you think that? I'm not an outdoorsy person. Remember when you talked me into camping on our honeymoon? We spent a week in a tent in Canada and it poured rain the whole time. All our food got wet, and I caught poison ivy even though we never went outside. The doctor said he never saw poison ivy that bad. I was miserable.

HAROLD

I know, but you can't judge from one experience—that's not what camping's really like. I know you'll enjoy it more when we do it again.

LOUISE

I don't want to do it again.

HAROLD

We just didn't do it the right way. When you see all the improvements they've made in camping gear, you'll be amazed. As a matter of fact, I wasn't going to tell you this, but your anniversary present has a bit of an outdoorsy theme.

LOUISE
What are you talking about?

HAROLD
Camping gear! I got us the latest alpine tent, all the cooking gear, a water purifier, thermal insulated sleeping bags, a little heater for when it gets below zero at night (although these new sleeping bags are so toasty!), and everything else we'll need to take some terrific camping trips! I ordered it all online, and it's being delivered tomorrow.

LOUISE
That's my anniversary present?

HAROLD
Yes! Isn't it great? Oh I know I could have bought you some jewelry, but this was much more practical—although it cost as much as a diamond necklace, let me tell you.

LOUISE
How much did you pay?

HAROLD

Oh, five thousand dollars, give or take a few bucks. Nothing but the best for my sweetheart! And it was a bargain—you ought to see how much people can spend on gear. Camping has become quite an expensive pastime!

LOUISE

You spent $5,000 on camping equipment without talking to me about it?

HAROLD

It's the latest in high-tech camping. And look, I'm willing to compromise on this, Louise. You can make all the plans. We'll go anywhere in the world you want! After all, 35 years is worth celebrating in a big way.

LOUISE

You're not listening, Harold. I hate camping! I don't like bugs, and feeling cold, and getting wet, and catching poison ivy, and boiling water for my tea on a little stove, and all the other aggravation that goes along with it. I don't like wilderness, Harold—human beings evolved so we could get away from all that, and now you want to take me back to it? No way!

HAROLD

That's the trouble with you—no sense of adventure.

LOUISE

I have a sense of adventure—it just doesn't involve going back to the Stone Age. My sense of adventure is about finding a piece of art or an antique or a restaurant in some little out of the way place that nobody has heard of. My sense of adventure comes from meeting new people and learning new things. I also happen to like sleeping in a bed, Harold, not on the ground.

HAROLD

I can't believe you're being so unreasonable. I thought when we finally got Tommy out of the house we could—

LOUISE

We could go camping in the woods? It's clear you haven't been listening for 35 years. That was never my plan.

HAROLD

I thought you could be more adaptable, Louise.

LOUISE

Why can't you be the one who's adaptable? Why does it have to be me? You're being pig-headed, Harold.

HAROLD

Maybe I ought to go camping by myself, then!

LOUISE

Yes, maybe you ought to. Go sleep in the woods by yourself in your damn thermal sleeping bag!

HAROLD

And you can just take your damn trip to Europe!

TOMMY
enters with Sarah

Hi Mom, hi Dad! I hope you don't mind that we got here early!

HAROLD
embarrassed

Tommy! Uh no, not a problem. Come right in! And there's the lovely Sarah! How are you, Sarah?

SARAH

I'm, er, fine. Are you sure we're not intruding? I told Tommy we shouldn't come too early.

HAROLD

Not at all! They're not intruding, are they Louise? I was just telling Louise how great it is that you can join us for our anniversary dinner.

TOMMY

We wouldn't miss it, Dad!

SARAH

It's such a big anniversary, and we wanted to help you celebrate. You seem to have the perfect marriage!

LOUISE

Perfect? I don't know about that—

HAROLD

Ha, ha, nothing is really perfect in this world, but Louise and I, well our marriage comes pretty close. But I don't want to brag, that's not our style. Why don't you two sit down and I'll get you something to drink. We have time before our restaurant reservation. How about some champagne?

LOUISE

Harold, we don't have any champagne in the house.

HAROLD

Oh, yes we do! As a matter of fact, we have Dom Perignon! I found it in the basement, way back behind some boxes. It was a wedding gift from my boss, and if you remember we thought we lost it years ago. Well, it was down there in the basement all along! I put it in the basement refrigerator last night, so it should be just the right temperature by now.

LOUISE

I hate to disappoint you dear, but it probably went flat. That's a long time for champagne to go unopened.

HAROLD

Nonsense! I'm sure it will be delicious. Kids, get ready for something special! I'll just go downstairs and get it. Be right back!

SARAH
To Louise

This is so exciting, your 35th anniversary! It's wonderful to see a long marriage like yours.

What's your secret?

LOUISE
My secret? Well, I'd say it's listening. Yes, it's so important to pay attention to what your spouse is saying.

Suddenly she has an idea

And speaking of that, do you know what my spouse just told me?

SARAH & TOMMY
What?

LOUISE
"We'll go anywhere in the world you want." That's a direct quote. He's letting me plan an anniversary trip anywhere in the world! It was quite a surprise but I've already decided where I want to go—a two week trip to Europe. Paris, Rome, Florence, Venice—all the cities I love. Isn't that wonderful?

TOMMY
Wow, I bet that's expensive! It doesn't sound like Dad.

LOUISE

Oh, your father loves to spend money on important things like anniversary gifts.

SARAH

What a wonderful husband!

LOUISE

Yes, he is. And Sarah, I have a great idea—you can help me plan this right now. We'll get the plane tickets, the hotel reservations, and everything will be finalized before we go out to dinner! Tommy, bring my laptop over—it's on the chair over there.

SARAH

Sarah sits down next to Louise. Tommy brings the laptop over and gives it to Louise, then Harold enters, glumly holding the champagne bottle.

HAROLD

I opened it and there was no fizz at all. It's as flat as tap water.

SARAH

You're such a wonderful husband, Mr. Wilson.

HAROLD

Me? Well, thank you!

SARAH

And it's so nice you're taking Mrs. Wilson on such a lovely trip.

HAROLD

Trip? What trip?

TOMMY

It's so great. Mom just told us about your anniversary trip.

HAROLD

Our anniversary trip you say?

LOUISE

Yes, dear. The trip you promised me for our anniversary. Where you said I could go anywhere I wanted? We're going to Europe.

HAROLD

Europe?

SARAH

And what an itinerary, Mr. Wilson—Paris, Rome, Florence, Venice—the most romantic places in the world—what a beautiful idea for an anniversary trip! You certainly are a romantic!

HAROLD
Well, I, uh—

SARAH
It's such a wonderful example of true love.

HAROLD
Um, yes.

SARAH
You just don't see enough of that in today's world. It's sad but true. But this—it gives me faith in the whole idea of marriage.

HAROLD
Right. Uh, don't mention it. Yes, it's nice to have these things to look forward to far off in the future. Of course, plans can change, and—

LOUISE
Oh, Sarah and I are going to plan the whole thing right now—we're booking the hotels, buying the airline tickets—the whole nine yards. No time like the present, right Sarah?

HAROLD

But our dinner reservation! Don't we have to leave for our reservation now?

TOMMY

pulls out his cell phone

No problem, Dad, I'll just text the restaurant and ask them to hold our table for another half hour. There, it's done. Oh, and they just replied and said it's fine.

LOUISE

Isn't technology wonderful?

HAROLD

(Through gritted teeth). Yes. It. Is.

TOMMY

Gee Dad, I'm sorry about the champagne. Now you can't make your toast.

HAROLD

Sighs

Yes, no toast. *(gets an idea)* Wait a minute! I'll be right back.

He runs out.

TOMMY

What's he doing?

LOUISE

I have no idea, dear.

Harold comes back with champagne glasses filled with water, and he gives them out.

LOUISE

What's this?

HAROLD

Plain old tap water! Who needs champagne for a toast? It's not what's in the glass, it's the words you say that count the most. I'd like to make a toast to saying yes. If there's one thing I've learned in 35 years of marriage, it's that you have to be ready to say yes. Here's to 35 years of marriage to my lovely Louise—I said yes 35 years ago, and I'm so glad I did. To yes!

EVERYONE

To yes!

THE END

Did you like this book? I encourage you to write a short review on Amazon. Reader reviews are extremely important in today's publishing world, and I'd be eternally grateful if you'd take the time to write one (no matter what rating you give the book). Thanks!

You can discover more of my books on Amazon

https://www.amazon.com/John-McDonnell/e/B004AXGYHQ/ref=dp_byline_cont_pop_ebooks_1

John McDonnell's Website

https://www.johnfmcdonnell.com

McDonnell Writing Facebook Page

https://www.facebook.com/JohnMcDonnellsWriting

Want to give me your feedback? Send an email: mcdonnellwrite@gmail.com

Printed in Great Britain
by Amazon

14940171R00129